Kendo, Inherited Wisdom
and Personal Reflections

Kendo,
Inherited Wisdom and
Personal Reflections
Geoff Salmon

R3THINK PRESS

First published in 2013 by Rethink Press
(www.rethinkpress.com)

© Copyright Geoff Salmon

Front cover design by Katsuya Masagaki (www.katsuya.co.uk)

Foreword

This collection of the most popular posts from www.kendoinfo.net contains 52 articles on various aspects of kendo technique and attitude. Its subjects include training methods and kendo techniques as well as the attitudes and philosophies that make kendo a lifetime's pursuit for many people. It highlights some of the differences between kendo training in Japan and other parts of the globe and includes some light-hearted commentary on this martial sport from the author.

This compilation also includes some direct translations of the words of the late Matsumoto sensei Hanshi kyudan and includes insights and advice gleaned from some of the leading contemporary kendo teachers including Inoue Yoshihiko sensei, Chiba Masashi sensei, Sumi Masatake sensei and Iwadate Saburo sensei.

This is not an instruction manual. It is offered with the intention of entertaining and stimulating those interested in the art of kendo.

Contents

The Aim of Kendo

by Matsumoto Toshio, Hanshi Kyudan

MATSUMOTO SENSEI

This document was written in Japanese by Matsumoto Toshio sensei and translated in 1976 by Yamamoto Hisami. The original translation was for my benefit; and at the time Matsumoto sensei was not satisfied that the document was of a high enough standard to put his name to. Unfortunately, neither the author nor the original translator are with us today and, feeling that this document is worth sharing with other kendo enthusiasts, I have taken the liberty of rewriting it in more colloquial English. Any errors and inconsistencies are mine.

The aim of swordsmanship in ancient days was to overcome opponents through the application of sword techniques and physical power, but this has changed with the progression of time. Even so, kendo was born from the art of fighting with swords and even though today it is played with bamboo swords, it cannot be said to be kendo if it is practised without the concept of being a fight with real swords. You must train for kendo with the understanding that if you cannot cut your opponent, he is going to cut you. In other words, in its essence, kendo must be practised with the extreme instability of mind that would occur if you were facing life or death.

There is no doubt that the art of kendo is to strike down your opponents and not to be struck down by them. However, in order to be always ready to give an instant strike without missing any proper chances to attack whilst still keeping a perfect defence position, you must master the techniques and skills of kendo. These however, can only be well performed when you maintain a calmness of mind which enables you to fully display your trained technique.

Therefore, it is the true aim of kendo practice not only to try to improve your technique, but also to train your mind and spirit to find the rightness of mind ("no mind"

/ mushin), so that your mind, which is the source of the technique, will not be bound by anything.

In the practice of kendo, it is most desirable that the training of mind and technique should always progress hand in hand. A strike should not be made recklessly, but you should strike when the opponent's mind is disturbed. Ineffective or hurried strikes are the causes of self destruction. The following are cited as good chances to attack:

1. Not to attack when your opponent is in replete condition, but try to attack when he is unaware and off-guard

2. Attack just before your opponent starts to take (initiates) his action

3. Attack when your opponent is settled

4. Attack when your opponent has exhausted his tricks

5. Attack at the time that your opponent has doubt in his mind

6. Urge your opponent's action and attack the created off-guard position

The three points that would be inexcusable to overlook are:

1. Just when your opponent initiates his action

2. When your opponent parries

3. When your opponent has exhausted his tricks

These are again times when your opponent is off-guard.

In kendo there are four mental states that must be overcome. These are dread, fright, doubt and perplexity – all of which are disturbed states of mind. When your mind is disturbed, your posture is also disturbed leaving you off-guard and allowing your opponent the chance to attack. Unless you are constantly in full spirit, keeping your mind calm and open, you cannot instantly strike your opponent off-guard, even when his spirit is no longer alert. If your mind is innocent (free of preconception), you can see through all your opponent's actions and strike freely without any hesitation, catching every available chance.

In Zen Buddhism, "voidness" is sometimes explained as "The true way of life is to always keep your normal mind". It is considered to be a state of mind which has no preconceived ideas, free and active without being bound by egotistic interests. You may think that it is extremely difficult to have an innocent mind and that it is the highest condition of mind and impossible to attain, but one who is experienced in kendo to a considerable degree should achieve a similar mental state

When reflecting on a keiko or shiai, one sometimes realises that he has unconsciously made a very fine strike, although such experiences are rare. It is because the perpetrator was in full spirit and "innocent", enabling an unintended and unaware strike. You must make every effort to increase these opportunities.

From a reversed perspective you need to maintain an undisturbed "ordinary" mind in order to defend well without being struck by your opponent. To keep disturbances from your mind you must:

1. Master the basic forms of kendo

2. Understand and appreciate the theory of kendo and try to improve kendo techniques

3. Have a firm belief that you are perfectly invincible against any assault

As stated above, the ultimate way of learning kendo is, both in attack and in defence, to have a constant ordinary state of mind through the theory of the way of kendo. I believe that it is a virtue of kendo to bring to our social lives this developed ordinary mind, rich and level without egotistic interest and emotional influences.

Making best use of such an attitude, you will be able to take good advice from other people and clearly differentiate right and wrong, allowing for effective conduct in your job and at the same time working towards self perfection.

2

Kendo no kata – the deeper meaning

The spring grading examinations are looming and I am getting a number of requests to teach kata or to act as a kata training partner for candidates. I mentioned in an earlier post on the subject, that I share the guilt of many kendoka in not practising kata often enough. When I do make the effort, I realise that kata is a superb vehicle to demonstrate not just the whole range of kendo technique, but it also teaches seme, distance and timing.

Kata, in the right frame of mind when you can truly harmonise with your partner, is a joy. I have had two experiences of kata that have had a profound effect on my understanding of kendo and the way I view the world. The first was quite a few years ago when I was preparing for the 5th dan grading in Japan. A sensei from Nishinomiya in Hyogo arranged for the two of us to perform kata privately in the local hachiman shrine as dawn was breaking. The second, more recently, was again a one on one session. This time with a friend who was practising for the opening kata at a taikai in Nara. We did this with mogito in Uegaki sensei's Taisho period dojo in Yoshino, with Uegaki sensei correcting every move.

Both these experiences were made special as much by the spirituality of the location as by the quality of my opponent. I was also fortunate to attend a kata seminar in Osaka, given by the late Ikeda sensei who explained in detail the riai of kendo no kata, demonstrating the kodachi section at almost a running pace to show that the possessor of a short sword would do his utmost to close the distance with an opponent using a longer weapon. This riai (or the theory or reason for each movement), is what makes kata meaningful.

To give an indication of the deeper meaning of kendo no kata, I quote from the paper submitted by Kensei Hiwaki of Tokyo International University, entitled "A breakthrough in the dilemma of war or peace – The teachings of kendo". The author borrows from the physical description of the kata from Hiroshi Ozawa in "Kendo the definitive guide" and the mental aspects from Yoshihiko Inoue in "Nippon kendo no kata no ichi kosatsu".

In this section the author discusses the lesson taught by ippon me, the first technique of the kata:

The first kata begins with jodan no kamae. The person on the right assumes the role of teacher (uchidachi) and the one on the left the role of student (shidachi) in the training for kata. As the teacher executes a frontal attack with an indomitable fighting spirit, the student parries (sic) and delivers a frontal strike. In this kata exercise, both the teacher and the student attack each other from the "overhead" posture implying a clash of justice against justice. The first kata is meant to teach that one defeats the other with the difference of relative skill cultivation that corresponds to the laws of nature.

The author goes on to explain that,

The first lesson in kendo means training for the self-acquirement of the physical movement and mental attitude, as well as the cultivation for the self-manifestation of justice. In addition to the self-manifestation, the first kata teaches the importance of repentance for the killing. In real combat, the loser dies and the winner who survives must have repentance. This mental attitude in part represents the assertion of zanshin.

He then illustrates the meaning of the second and third kata in the same fashion. Of course this is a far more profound view of kata than we often take, but it certainly starts to give meaning to what are often meaningless actions based on "one two three, yah-toh".

3

Fudōshin 不動心

Achieving fudōshin is one of the long term objectives of kendo practice. Literally meaning "immovable mind", fudōshin is the ability to remain calm and imperturbable under pressure. Fudōshin is symbolised by the Shingon Buddhist deity Fudō myōō, one of the five "Kings of Wisdom" and a patron of warriors.

Fudōshin is the protection against the "shikai" or four sicknesses of kendo: surprise, fear, doubt and confusion. A kendoka should not lose his composure under pressure or provocation. In practical terms this means not flinching under the pressure of a sudden strong attack, or reacting hastily to a feint. It equally means not losing your temper when reacting to off-target blows or physical contact and in having the courage and commitment to finish an attack once you initiate it.

For all but the most experienced kendoka, this sounds worthy, but simplistic and hard to achieve. However, the ability to approach kendo practice with an immovable mind, even for a small proportion of the time, makes for immeasurable progress. Unfortunately there is no instant solution, nor is there a way to reach fudōshin by reading or thinking about it. Like most aspects of kendo, the goal is reached through repeated kihon practice.

Breaking it down into its components, one can see that uchikomi geiko and kakarigeiko focus the attacker on striking the target without fear of failure or counter attack. Drills to repetitively practise oji-waza help you meet your opponents' attack without fear. Butsukarigeiko helps build a robust attacking spirit, which is not put off or offended by the occasional knock. Kirikaeshi develops the ability to breathe whilst attacking continuously, allowing you to keep the pressure on without being overwhelmed by your opponent. In fact, these basic drills should be the building blocks for your kendo and jigeiko no more than the opportunity to polish and test the skills you have developed.

Of course, kendo is finally about the interaction between two people and the outcome of shiai is dictated by your comparative levels of skill and mental strength, but you only strengthen these through repeated basic training. There is no quick fix, but just a tip: if your mind, body and the tip of your shinai continuously move forward, you are going in the right direction.

4

Thoughts on maai
prompted by Chiba sensei

There are some very complex English language explanations of maai available on the internet. Many of them talk about the duality of time and distance inherent in the word. One of the simplest descriptions of the terminology is to be found in the All Japan Kendo Federation's *Japanese-English Dictionary of Kendo*, where "ma" is translated as the interval in time and "maai" the physical distance between you and your opponent.

Having accepted the terminology, we are then treated by most writers to the differences between toi maai or toma, (long distance), issoku itto maai (one step, one sword distance) and chika maai, (close distance). All are, of course, very important aspects of kendo, but perhaps too much to think about if your question is simply, "which distance should I attack from?"

I was originally taught to penetrate the opponent's kensen by 15 centimetres, and if there was no chance to attack to try another 15cm. Still unable to make an opening, then go back to safe distance and start again. This was useful advice but perhaps a little too prescriptive and "one size fits all". Chiba sensei, on the other hand, talks about "moving as far as you need to into the opponent's distance to break his kamae and to arrive at a point where you can comfortably strike the datotsu-bu with the correct part of the shinai in one step, whilst retaining good posture."

This is logical and not unique to Chiba sensei. A number of famous kendo teachers have, over the years, voiced thoughts along the lines of "everyone has their own distance".

So, in essence we are talking about your ideal "one step one cut" distance, which means you have to be in a position to push off from the left foot and, in one step, cut the correct part of the target. This distance is by no means fixed. We are all different – our own height, weight, leg and arm length, age and muscle condition will govern the distance we can cover. Remember that your opponent's kote is closer than his men and that dou is further away. Also remember that the distance for oji-waza is closer, as your opponent is moving forward at the same time; so you need only the smallest of forward movements to make a successful strike.

Like many elements of kendo, the secret of success depends on sharp footwork and you need to practise to ensure that you can vary the distance you cover to suit the opportunity. Chiba sensei suggested a drill where you start from close up and experiment to find your own perfect distance. I would recommend this as a useful part of kihon practice.

5

"A feather in a hurricane"

Without the benefit of a private dojo for toshikoshi geiko, my first practice of the New Year took place yesterday. This hatsugeiko was a great way to get back into the swing of kendo and, with my wrist injury now mending, I am once again able to call on some oji waza to use against my fitter, faster juniors.

Perhaps because of the holiday break, or maybe because it is a reflective time of year, a number of people asked me to help evaluate their keiko. The common theme was that we all seemed to be operating at a single rhythm, by which I mean that there was no real differentiation between the speed of approach, attack and follow through. This could, of course, be attributed to a surfeit of Christmas pudding, but more likely the cause is just general tension and inability to relax.

Many years ago, I was given some advice by the late Kikuchi Koichi sensei, former Vice President of the BKA and more recently of Shibuya dojo, that the feeling in kendo should be "like a feather in a hurricane". This has been a constantly memorable image, signifying to me that kendo should be light and flexible but driven by a great elemental force. What sets great kendo players apart is the ability to instantly transform from a totally relaxed state to explosive movement.

Most of us will never achieve this, but there are certainly ways in which we can get closer to the ideal. Good posture and balance, and a relaxed, flexible kamae are all necessities. Correct footwork too is essential, with the ability to drive off from the left foot as soon as you see the opportunity. Most importantly the cut itself must be done with relaxed shoulders, elbows and wrists. If you use too much shoulder power, it makes your attack heavy and slow. The feeling on making the attack should be as if you are being pulled upward and forward, accelerating through the strike into zanshin.

This is all very easy to describe but very difficult to do. The ability to relax, particularly in stressful situations such as shiai and shinsa, needs strict mental as well as physical preparation. You need to control your breathing and put aside the kendo sicknesses of surprise, fear, doubt and perplexity. Whilst the ideal of "a feather in a hurricane" may not be achievable, you may avoid looking more like a pudding in a blizzard.

6

Chiba sensei's advice on chudan kamae and cutting motion

CHIBA SENSEI

Chiba sensei is back in the UK for his annual visit. He has an unerring ability to quickly spot what needs fixing and to offer a remedy. After two dojo visits for keiko, he reached the conclusion that many UK kendoka suffer from the lack of coordinated ki-ken-tai-itchi. This stems from a number of timing problems, but mainly from using too much shoulder power and leaning in, causing the right foot to come up rather than forward.

Over the weekend, he then ran a two day seminar. Using a series of drills that progressed through the range of shikake and oji waza at different speeds and distances, he made people work on developing a natural kamae and cutting motion to eliminate this problem. The theory is quite simple: that you should relax your arms and shoulders in chudan leaving your inner arms close to the body so that you cannot see daylight between your inner arms and your dou. Your left hand should be at navel height and turned in at an angle where you can easily support the weight of the shinai. Your right hand should be held at a relaxed angle without being forced, so that you can move the shinai easily. The grip from both hands comes from the little and ring fingers only.

You should step into your own, one-step cutting distance with a feeling of seme, and at the right time you should lift the shinai, bending your elbows and wrists in a natural fashion. How high you lift the shinai depends on you. If you are an experienced kendoka you should be able to cut in a very small movement. It needs to be bigger a motion if you are less experienced. The key point is that the final part of the motion with your wrists is what gives the strike its "snap" and if your wrists are supple enough, you should be able to cut from almost a standing start. As Chiba sensei has said in the past, when you strike men, you should do so with the intention of cutting through to the chin.

In terms of getting the foot movement part of the equation right, you should not move your right foot before you start the strike; however, just before you do so, bend the right knee slightly. Not only can this provoke your opponent to move, it aligns your leg so that when you make a fumikomi stamp, you will painlessly hit the floor with the flat of your foot rather than risk bruising your heel.

As simple as the theory might be, for many of us it will take quite a few hours in the dojo before we can put it into practice.

Tenouchi

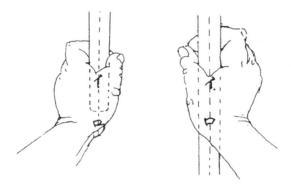

I touched on tenouchi in an early post on holding the shinai and in my report on Chiba sensei's first UK seminar. I make no excuses for posting about it again because it is an important aspect of kendo and, in many cases, the final piece of the puzzle that decides whether or not a technique results in ippon.

Tenouchi translates simply as "the inside of the hand" and in kendo means the squeezing action of both hands at the point of striking. If you squeeze too hard or too early, the point of the shinai will not extend forward sufficiently to strike the target correctly and crisply. In some kendojo, people were, and maybe still are, taught to wring the shinai between both hands at the point of cutting. Unfortunately this has the effect of causing the point of the shinai to rise on impact, so it actually defeats the purpose of using it as an aid to finish the cut correctly.

Like every other component of kendo, tenouchi should be relaxed and natural. Rather than create an artificial action at the end of your cutting swing, you should start the movement holding the shinai correctly. That is, with the end of the tsuka fitting into the heel of your left hand, the little finger and ring finger applying slight pressure, with the middle, index finger and thumb barely making contact. For the right hand the grip is the same, but if anything lighter and the knuckle of the forefinger should lightly brush the tsuba. If this is uncomfortable, chances are your tsuka is too long. I cannot overemphasise that your grip should be light. If someone tries to pull your shinai forward out of your hand, it should slide forward without protest or friction. A further key point is that your wrists should turn in slightly, so that the centre of the V formed by thumb and forefinger of each hand should be at a 90 degree angle to the ground.

Holding the shinai in this way, you should aim to cut through the men to chin level and kote through the thickness of the wrist and squeeze lightly with the little and index fingers after the point of impact. You should not change your grip at any stage of the cut.

Kigurai

Vincent Long of the Irish Kendo Federation asked for some help in explaining Kigurai to his students. At first, this appeared to be a fairly straightforward exercise but, as with everything related to kendo, the more you think about it, the more complicated it becomes.

In everyday Japanese it means "pride" and has a slightly negative connotation – it could be taken to mean haughtiness. In kendo there are various definitions ranging from the late Ando sensei's "loftiness of mind" to the ZNKR dictionary's "the strength or commanding presence derived from confidence acquired through repeated practice". When you break down the original characters to "mind" and "grade" you can see the logic behind these more positive kendo definitions.

I am starting to get rapidly out of my comfort zone when thinking about the subtle difference between "kihaku" *strength of mind,* "fukaku" *depth* and kigurai, but to get back to Vinnie's question, kigurai can mean confidence, grace, the ability to dominate your opponent through strength of character. Kigurai can also be seen as fearlessness or a high level of internal energy. What it is not is posturing, self-congratulating or show-boating.

Most of us have at some time seen Kurosawa's *Seven Samurai*. In the film, one of the protagonists gets involved in a dual with bokken in which his opponent loudly insists that his men attack had beaten the nuki dou of the quietly confident hero. Forced into a replay with katana, our hero modestly repeats the process, watching the baddy's two halves go off in different directions. He then, without showing any emotion, puts his sword away and walks on. This to me is a great example of kigurai.

Kigurai becomes a required element to display in grading examinations from 4th dan upwards. This underlines the ZNKR's view that kigurai can only be built on extensive keiko. You may well be able to explain the concept, but without putting in the thousands of hours of required practice, it is unlikely that anyone can display kigurai.

However, anyone can start to build it from day one. Taking dojo etiquette seriously, making the most of seiza and mokuso and repeatedly practicing kihon with a level mind and good posture are ways to lay foundations for the splendid kigurai that you will naturally show in your yondan examination.

9

Kendo footwork for beginners

I do not often teach beginners, but I do notice from time to time that individuals who are now well past the first stages of learning kendo still have problems in making correct fumikomi.

Teaching at the last seminar in Ireland was illuminating as there were a number of new kendoka who were working very hard to establish the basis of good kendo foot movement. This made me reflect on how important it is to perfect the basics before you can move on to learn more complex kendo technique.

Certainly from a western perspective, the concept of suri ashi, (sliding feet) and okuri ashi, (moving the foot facing the direction you move in) is alien: We learn to walk heel-toe, lifting the leg from the knee and transferring the weight from the back to the front of the foot. Kendo foot movement developed in Japan at a time when people were used to wearing geta and zori and needed to slide their feet forward.

The repercussions of heel-toe walking are still obvious, with many beginners instinctively pulling from the front foot rather than pushing from the back foot.

The key points to remember are that the back leg should be tense with the heel only slightly raised (just 15 degrees). The knee of the front leg should be slightly bent and the foot should be parallel to the ground, as if a thin sheet of paper were between it and the floor. In the words of Matsumoto Toshio sensei, the movement should be "like a cat walking".

Everyone is taught that the toes of the left foot should be in line with the heel of the right and that there should be a fist's distance in width between them. I think that this can vary. If you have sufficient leg power, then there is no reason why your feet should not be further apart. The width between them should also depend on your own body shape and size. What I am trying to say is that your feet should be in a position that feels comfortable and stable.

In my view, the most important element is hikitsuke, the process of drawing the back foot to its relative position with the front foot as soon as you move forward or make fumikomi to strike. In this way you maintain balance and the ability to move forward instantly.

Tame

The two comments on "tame" received in response to my post about Chiba sensei's seminar were in line with the reaction of many people at the event, who had difficulty in understanding the concept of "tame".

I mentioned this to Chiba sensei at the meal after his farewell practice, and his reply was that "you should approach the opponent in the spirit of, 'I am cutting now' and wait for his or her reaction to determine which target to strike."

This is a good explanation, but for the benefit of readers who are not familiar with "tame", let me add what little I can on the subject.

Firstly "tame" is an extension of seme. I have written about this before, but the act of moving into your opponent's distance or inviting them into yours is seme. Seme, and the technique that follows it should not, however, be continuous. If it were that would show premeditation on the attacker's part to hit, for example, men, when his or her opponent could well react differently and show another target.

"Tame" is the interval between approaching and striking where you determine your opponent's next step and choose your target. Of course this makes it all sound very leisurely, where that is far from the case.

So practically, you step in and staying relaxed, maintain your pressure and readiness to attack. Your chudan, (explaining "tame" from jodan is beyond my ability), should be firmly fixed on your opponent's centre. You need to maintain the tension in your left leg so that you can push forward instantly and contain your breath in your abdomen so that you can move explosively with strong kiai. As soon as your opponent moves – attack. This could be with any shikake waza if he or she breaks their kamae, or with oji waza if they choose to attack. Of course, they may choose to do neither, in which case the only solution is to move back to safe distance and start all over again.

I hope this helps. For further information there is a translation of an article on seme and tame by Lorenzo Zago on the BKA website, or better still, find a clip of Chiba sensei on YouTube and watch how he does it.

11

The Nito kodachi conundrum

I was happily browsing through the new *Official Guide for Kendo Instruction*, nodding sagely at the explanations of things I knew, when I reached the section on yuko datotsu. Having refereed internationally on many occasions and attended all the regional referee training courses, I like to think that I have a fairly clear idea of what constitutes ippon. My confidence started to waiver a little when I read the description of yuko datotsu for nito, particularly the explanation of ippon for the shoto.

Forgive me if I do not give the exact quote, as I am travelling without the book at the moment, but to score with the shoto the daito must be holding down the opponent's shinai whilst the arm holding the daito (the long one) is fully extended. Just to clarify this point, it means that the opponent's shinai is being suppressed at a distance equating to the length of the arm plus a 38 shinai when you strike with the shoto (the little one). I am very far from being a nito expert. I have never tried it and have no intention of doing so, but if I am not missing something, the rule makes it impossible to score with the shoto unless the player has a two metre arm or a telescopic kodachi.

I wrote about nito before and mentioned that I have never seen ippon given to a kodachi strike. I have also heard a variety of explanations from referee instructors and shinpancho about the difficulty of making yuko datotsu with the kodachi, because nito is "different from mainstream kendo", but this makes it patently clear that the shoto is not meant for scoring with.

12

Tsuki – fact or fiction?

Back in 2009 I wrote a piece about tsuki. Since then, I have continued to see the occasional YouTube video of this technique resulting in brilliant ippon in the All Japan Championships, but I never see the technique practised.

I have enjoyed keiko on four continents (I still hope to get to Australia), and have hardly ever seen anyone doing tsuki drills. I have witnessed numerous university practices and the occasional police tokuren session in Japan where tsuki has been ignored. This begs the question – how do those athletes who excel in tsuki get to be so good at it?

There are lots of implicit embargos on tsuki. It should not be done by beginners or children, or used by more experienced players against the same. It is also thought to be impolite to do tsuki against a senior teacher. This does actually make sense, as keiko between instructor and student tends to take the form of hikitategeiko, where the senior partner subtly makes openings for the junior. In this situation it would be extremely rude to charge in with a heart-stopping tsuki when sensei kindly opens for you to attack men.

There is also a feeling, although I have never heard anything definitive on this point, that tsuki should not be attempted in grading examinations. Having watched the hachidan shinsa five or six times, I have only seen tsuki from one individual who has become a minor legend. At every grading, his reputation causes a knot of anticipation where the watchers go through a "will he, won't he?" speculation. Every time I have seen him in action, his very impressive tsuki emerges before the end of his second tachiai. I am a long way from being able to understand whether this is the reason for him not getting through to the niji shinsa, but his kendo looks pretty good to me.

Perhaps I am painting too negative a picture. Tsuki is included in most courses and seminars, but normally its inclusion is brief and it seems to be there as the token fourth technique. Nevertheless the kendo world seems to be split between those who can't do tsuki and those who excel at it. It is probably the result of my over-active imagination, but I have the suspicion that those who can spend their nights away from prying eyes practising tsuki in the dark.

13

Kendo Training – frequency and intensity

A regularly asked question is, "How often should I train to gain maximum improvement in my kendo?" My honest answer would be, "At least three times a week." Once a week and you are not going to make any real progress, twice and you may improve slightly if you already have a strong grounding, but train three times a week and you are able to reinforce your good habits and learn new skills.

This is, however, an unrealistic goal for many people. Busy working lives, family commitments and the lack of local dojo often make the ideal training schedule untenable.

The other part of the equation is how you use your time in the dojo. If you turn up, shoot the breeze for half an hour then enjoy one or two leisurely jigeiko before retiring to the pub, you are not going to improve much, even if you train on a daily basis. To my mind, an intense hour's practice with at least half of it dedicated to rigorous kihon, including drills, kirikaeshi and kakarigeiko, with the remaining time dedicated to jigeiko, is the ideal session. Most Japanese instruction manuals constantly refer to "correct technique" and "in full spirit", which reading between the lines suggests that you should do it to the best of your ability and with your utmost energy. Of course the other element that significantly adds to the value of your training is to do it under the watchful eye of a good instructor, one who can help you correct mistakes and praise you when you get it right.

Elite kendoka in Japan often train twice a day with a break at midday for a meal and a nap. This normally happens five days a week with the weekends reserved for competition. There are also a number of happily retired kendoka who attend morning and evening practice five or six days a week, but for working amateurs with a mortgage to pay and kids to feed, this remains the stuff of dreams.

There has been some recent debate on a number of kendo groups about the value of cross training and I honestly believe that anything that increases stamina, speed and flexibility has got to be worth doing. On the other hand, no amount of running, cycling or swimming is going to improve your kendo technique.

You can of course train at home. Suburi and footwork exercises can be practised in most places. However, looking at my own history of smashed light fittings, annoyed neighbours and a dispute with my former Japanese landlords over floor damage, I would counsel caution.

14

Kaeshi dou

As most people who practise with me know, I like kaeshi dou. Trying to teach it, though, is not a simple matter. To be honest, I have not seen many kendoka below 4th dan attempt it successfully.

Dou generally is a difficult technique. Against correct chudan, there is rarely an opportunity for tobikomi dou. Hiki dou works if your opponent is intent on covering his or her men; some younger competitors do a good job with gyaku dou, but the most common successful application of dou is as an oji technique, either nuki or kaeshi dou.

The two are not dissimilar, but I much prefer kaeshi dou as the blocking and returning motion allow you to hit dou whilst you are directly in front of your opponent. In my view, there are a number of factors that are key to making a successful kaeshi dou:

- Make sure that you approach the technique with an attacking mind! Do not wait for your opponent to strike men and then react.

- Ensure your posture is correct, but with your balance just slightly forward.

- The block and strike should be one smooth, continuous movement.

- As with all oji waza, make sure the point of your shinai is going forward rather than lifting up and back.

- Hit dou whilst you are in front of your opponent and then move diagonally for your zanshin, do not hit after you have moved.

- Keep your left hand in the centre and only break your right hand grip as you move diagonally.

- Make sure you hit the side of the dou and do not just scrape across the front.

- Have correct hasuji, the bottom take and string should be at 45 degrees to the dou.

- Keep correct distance so that you hit with the datotsu bu.

All of these elements are important, but in my view, attacking mind is the most significant; pull you opponent in and make him attack in your space and timing.

Successful kaeshi dou takes a lot of work, but it is great when it comes off!

15

Kendo Attitude

I have had a few days rest from work and kendo due to a tummy bug, so am feeling a little more reflective than usual. I re-read an article by Inoue Yoshihiko sensei on Kendo and Love. In this very erudite article, Inoue sensei examines through kendo and Buddhist philosophy, the way we evolve through kendo training to make a positive contribution to society.

I do not consider myself remotely qualified to comment on teaching that is based on such a depth of practical and philosophical kendo knowledge, but I started to think whether or not we are starting to lose some of the spiritual and moral values of kendo along with the older generation of kendo teachers.

The fact that I am even writing this is indicative that I think we are, but that is from my perspective as a westerner who does not read Japanese. I suppose a question that has been at the back of my mind for a long time is – Was modern kendo formulated to foster a love of mankind (as the mission statement says), or did someone do a great job of creating a rationale for a now irrelevant form of sword play?

Having practised kendo for 40 years and with the firm intention of continuing to do so until I am no longer able, I do, of course, believe that I gain a great deal of mental and physical benefit from regular keiko, but it is impossible to say whether or not I am a better person for it.

Thanks to the internet, there is now much more English language kendo information available. Much of it is either news about kendo events or discussions on technique. What is missing is the philosophical element! This is probably due to the fact that most people putting information out on blogs and web sites, (me included), are not qualified to discuss the more esoteric aspects of kendo. There is also the Zen conundrum that you do not reach a state of "no mind" by thinking about it.

What does seem clear is that as kendo grows in popularity, particularly in the West, it is moving more towards sport and further away from traditional budo. By joining GAISF and with the requirement for drug testing at the 14WKC, we appear to be going in the same direction as Judo. My only hope is that through this evolution, we do not lose the discipline and *reiho* that separates kendo from other sports.

16

Explain shu ha ri

Most people taking a Kendo 3rd or 4th dan examination, where a written test is required, have been given this instruction. Most know that the answer is along the lines of "Shu is following one teacher", "Ha is breaking away to learn from others" and "Ri is establishing your own technique". OK, so given that our exam papers got marked, we would all pass, but I for one do not really understand the idea in practical terms.

There are a wide range of interpretations of this concept. "Shu" is pretty standard throughout them all. "Ha" varies in people's understanding, from seeking occasional help from other sensei, to leaving because you have outgrown your teacher. "Ri" is where the going gets tough... with explanations ranging from developing your own technique, to achieving "mu shin" or "no mind", to starting your own school.

It is interesting to see that with some other martial arts there is indeed a tendency for exponents to start their own schools. I have been suitably impressed by folk in their 20s and 30s who have achieved the rank of 10th or 12th dan, but this happens very rarely in Kendo. So clearly, few of us feel that we have reached the state of independence described by the more extreme meaning of "Ri".

As with most things in life, reality is less cut and dried than the theory. When you move on to "Ha" depends on your own level and that of your instructor and the depth of your relationship. Most people spread their wings gently, getting exposure to other teachers and new ideas at seminars and dojo visits. Those with aspirations to be strong shiai players usually get to attend national squad training and learn from coaches who can take them in that direction. I have heard of a few dojo leaders who expect their students to cut themselves off from other influences, but this is more often than not due to their own insecurity. I believe that once a kendoka has started to put his or her basics in place, he or she should try to learn as much as they can from as many people as possible. Having said that, it is good to have one special sensei or sempai, whose kendo you admire; who can give you advice based on deep knowledge of your kendo.

Overall, the process of improving in Kendo is one of interdependence. We learn from our seniors, our peers and our juniors, and if we are lucky enough we should be able to do all three. In Europe it does become more difficult to practise with seniors once you achieve the rank of 6th or 7th dan, but it is essential for one's development so the onus is on us to attend seminars, to make trips to practise with strong sensei and to ensure that our own kendo continues to grow.

As for "Ri", ask me again if I make hachidan.

17

Kihaku

I am trying to recover after four days and five nights of keiko with Sumi, Uegaki, Tashiro and Mori sensei.

We have just finished the annual Sumi seminar and by the final day there was a clearly visible improvement in the standard of Kendo for all participants. On the last day we held a grading examination to 5th dan level and, for the first time in my experience, 100 percent of the candidates passed. Of course the sensei worked on improving technique and posture and a lot of focus was put on correct footwork, but in my view, the biggest improvement made to everyone's kendo was through improved kiai.

I sincerely believe that in the UK we fail to teach beginners the importance of correct breathing and strong kiai, and that this has a major impact on the ability to finish waza correctly. Whereas if correct breath control is taught, the technicalities of finishing a technique tend to take care of themselves. Ideally, you should breathe in sharply and hold the air in your abdomen, then let out a small amount of this air as kiai or kakegoe before you enter cutting distance. You should then expel the rest of your breath sharply as a loud kiai at the point of striking. The difference between Kendo with and without this is similar to comparing a bout between two professional heavyweight boxers and a friendly slapping match.

As we get older and move up the grading ladder, kiai – or perhaps more appropriately kihaku *(the strength of our spirit)* – becomes more important. Muscle power decreases, so we need to resort to the strength of our mind or spirit to break an opponent's centre as we make an attack.

Watching people like Sumi sensei, who I have had the privilege of knowing for many years, you can see this transformation. Whereas 20 years ago I feared the speed of his attack, one is now transfixed by the strength of his ki.

So, coming back to our more immediate kiai concerns, what is the best way to train? The answer given loudly during the seminar was kirikaeshi. Deep breath, kakegoe, shomen and five yoko men with kiai without breathing in again – then stretch to shomen and seven yoko men. When you can do that, go on to the whole forward and back sequence in one breath. It hurts! But it will make one hell of a difference to your Kendo.

Training in Japan

18

It seems like half the current and recent former members of the British Kendo Squad are either in, planning to be, or have just returned from Japan. Cheap air travel and more frequent chances to make friends with Japanese kendoka before you go, make training in Japan an easier option than it used to be, but you still have to be resourceful enough to arrange a job or scholarship, or simply stash the funds to facilitate an extended stay.

Having done it in the past, I am frequently asked for advice, although things move on and kendoka currently in Japan can give a much more up to the minute picture than I can. Nevertheless, here are some general thoughts on kendo training in Japan, (I assume you have already worked out how you are going to live whilst you are there.)

Firstly, find a dojo where the training is in line with your kendo objectives. There is no point in training with elite police tokuren, (even if they would let you), if you are a middle-aged beginner. Equally, it would be a waste of opportunity for a high potential, national team member to train exclusively in a local kinpen dojo. Think about how hard you are prepared to train and how far you have to progress to be able to train on an equal footing to other members. The options are:

- High school / Junior high school dojo – fine if you are a pupil or teacher, but adults need to get some senior practice as well, or you become a professional motodachi.

- Local police station dojo – good place for beginners to practise from scratch with the kids. Do not get confused with other big police dojo like Sonezaki in Osaka.

- Local area kinpen dojo – again, often good for beginners, but all depends on the sensei who can range from 4th dan to hachidan.

- University dojo – vary in kendo reputation, but most have strong sensei and are very good places to develop good kihon habits and stamina, ideal if you are in roughly the same age bracket as the student population. Also a good place for senior OBs to practice oji waza.

- Company dojo – there are some really strong company dojo like Mitsubishi, Hankyu etc. and some that are more like social clubs.

- Private dojo – no two are alike and, again, the level of instruction varies enormously, but be ready for some serious one-on-one obligation with the shihan. Amongst these private dojo you sometimes come across those that have a particular interest in teaching kendo to non-Japanese and go as far as actively recruiting gaijin from other dojo. I see the advantage for people for whom the language is still a mystery, but they do not always have the highest level of instruction. Personally I take a "Groucho Club" (I would not join any club that wants me as a member) attitude to these establishments.

- Machi dojo – my favourite! Normally public-financed, central town dojo. Usually they have a good mix of grades and, depending on your level, you can normally find someone to take you under their wing. I spent three happy years in Osaka Shudokan.

- Central police dojo, like Keshicho or Osaka Fukei – great if you are advanced, young, fit and capable, or like me, old enough to be allowed to sit with a cold drink and watch the tokuren sweat for the first two hours and join in at the end for a leisurely keiko.

This is a not exhaustive but fairly daunting list of options. In my view the best way to select a dojo is to get in touch either directly, or through introduction, to any senior sensei you know in the area and trust their judgement in helping you find the right dojo. Once you are known, all sorts of other practice opportunities will present themselves.

Although the days of sitting on the dojo steps for three days before they let you in have passed, it is still not advisable to walk in off the street just because you hear kiai.

Shodan shinsa

Sometime back, I wrote a post on how to train for grading examinations. Having sat on the 4th and 5th dan panel in Brussels last week, and as I am scheduled to be an examiner for the Irish National Grading this coming week end, I thought it might be useful to highlight some of the points that the panel will be looking for on the day.

The purpose of the kendo grading examination is to allow you to demonstrate what you have learned and what you are capable of. It is unlikely that you will pull something out of the bag that you cannot do in your normal keiko. You need to have put in the quantity and quality of practice since your last grading to justify promotion. There are some people who treat the shinsa like a lottery – turn up often enough and your number will eventually come up. The chances are if you are doing the same things you did the last time you failed, you will fail again.

There are some excellent guides available to tell you step by step what to do for each grade, so this is just a quick overview of the points that catch an examiner's eye:

- Chakuso – clean unfaded hakama and keikogi. Hakama should be the right length, keikogi wrinkle free at the back. Bogu should be tied correctly with men himo of the correct length. Shinai should be in good condition with no protruding tsuru or nakayui and the tsuba should reach the bottom of the tsuka.

- Entry and exit – make sure that you understand the pattern for entering and crossing the shinsajo operating at that grading. Either watch the people before you, or if you are in the first group, ask.

- Sonkyo – bow correctly and make a strong confident sonkyo with a straight back. If you have knee problems tell the organisers and make an alternative salutation.

- Kamae – keep a strong kamae and make sure your left heel is off the ground.

- Full spirit – give yourself time to settle and make a strong kiai. Attack at the right opportunity, with full spirit. If your opponent counters or stops you with his shinai, do not let it break the force of your attack. Do not show emotion at, or acknowledge, your opponent's successful attack, just go on to take or make the opportunity for your own technique.

- Correct posture – keep your posture straight, do not duck to avoid being hit.

- Ki-ken-tai-itchi – remember that your hands and feet should work together.

- Seme – take the centre before you hit. If you can make your opponent move first and take debana waza, you should impress the panel.

- Zanshin – show good zanshin, do not showboat. Ensure that you turn and go forward to the correct distance after each attack.

- Most importantly – keep a clear mind and do not panic into attacking when there is no opportunity.

Good luck!

20

Kendo for senior citizens

Many kendo clubs advertise kendo as "suitable for people of all ages". Whilst I do not disagree with this, I think there are some serious caveats. Those lucky enough to start at a relatively young age have had the luxury of adapting kendo over the years and, to paraphrase Mochida sensei, allowing physical speed and strength to be replaced by technique and later by kizeme, based on strength of mind.

For people who take up kendo in late middle, or old age it is more difficult. There are exceptions, of course, but in most cases late starters lack the strength and flexibility to start with "young kendo" and it is impossible to cram decades of experience into a short beginner's course. Even seasoned kendoka can have problems after a long break from training.

I recently met an experienced Japanese player in his 30s who returned to kendo after a 10 year interval. Within minutes of reverting to university level footwork, he experienced Achilles tendon problems. So what should the more mature kenshi do to get the most gain without too much pain? Firstly, find a sympathetic instructor who understands the limitations of his students. Work on correct technique and cutting, and keep your posture correct. Try to make good fumikomi, but do not take such big steps that you strain your Achilles tendon. Always bring your left foot up quickly so the toe is in line with your right heel. Above all, relax. If you feel any sudden twinges, stop!

Being prudent, however, does not mean you should not practise with full spirit. It is not all bad news for us oldies. Someone told me about his dad who started at 60 and reached 5th dan without failing a single grading. I also have a friend who restarted after a 27 year break and reached 7th dan. So give it your best, but do not overdo it.

21

Sensei!

A friend who teaches Kendo in the UK's West Midlands told me about another local martial arts (not telling you which one) instructor who has the word sensei tattooed in large gothic letters on the back of his bald head. To my mind, not a good move. As well as the potential problem of a permanent redundant label if he gives up (a bit like tattooing a lover's name before you get chucked), it demonstrates a complete lack of understanding of what the word means.

Sensei is a courtesy title, so you can't apply it to yourself without looking, at best, confused. The literal meaning is "born before" and in normal Japanese society it is reserved for doctors, teachers, lawyers, politicians etc. If you are inside one of these groups, you would use the sensei title for senior or more experienced colleagues, whilst using san or kun as appropriate for juniors. In Japanese, sensei is a suffix, so the correct usage is after the person's name. It is Smith sensei, not sensei Smith. In kendo, sensei is usually reserved for 6th dan upwards and, even then, implies that he or she is older or more experienced. Fighters in the Kyoto Taikai are announced as such and such sensei, whereas younger elite kendoka are announced as so and so senshu in the All Japan Championships.

Sempai, too, gets a great deal of misuse. In its natural setting it indicates someone older, your senior at school or perhaps someone who started kendo, or at the dojo before you. In the UK, the term is applied to the person at the head of the student line who shouts instructions. Within the original meaning of sempai and kohai (the junior member of the partnership), relationships are fixed on a lifelong basis, regardless of eventual status changes. I was unfailingly amused to regularly hear an 80 year old addressing a 79 year old as kun and kimi (honorific normally used for young boys and "you" form used for children). Of course, both sides of the partnership have their own responsibility. The kohai normally packs and carries bogu bags and the sempai softens the blow of regular criticism by buying the drinks.

22

Stepping Back

I have always found that the easiest time to hit someone is when they step back. This is normally because in the act of doing so they break concentration and lose their kamae. Theoretically, if your chudan is correct it is impossible for an opponent to strike you. However, when you step backwards, particularly when you do so to avoid your opponent's pressure, you risk moving the point of your shinai from the centre. This is a perfect opportunity for your opponent to attack men. It is surprising that even strong players make this mistake. In most cases, they do so to give them sufficient distance to make their own attack, but once they are on the back foot it is relatively simple for the other party to take an extra step forward and strike.

It is not difficult to avoid this problem: simply do not step back. If you think about keeping the point of the shinai forward at all times it is easier to apply counter techniques and the worst that can happen is that you both move forward into tsubazeriai. Now you can move back safely into fighting distance, but do so watching your opponent and covering his shinai. Most importantly, ensure that you keep your left heel off the ground as, once your heel is planted, you are unable to move in any direction and again become an easy target.

I realise that this advice is taking a somewhat negative tone in being a list of things not to do. Looking at it in a more positive light, your objective is to keep moving forward. Constantly take the fight to your opponent's half of the court or practice area and break his or her posture and kamae by strongly stepping into their distance. When we talk about this, the question most often asked is, "What happens if your opponent also comes forward?" This does and will happen, but your mindset should be that you will dominate and, if you really believe that, the chances are that the other player will crumble under the pressure.

Different Paths

23

Despite the panic of trying to complete my December work load before Christmas, I am in a good mood. Mainly because I have just had my hachidan keiko fix, which should keep me going into the new year.

We were very fortunate to have Iwatate Saburo sensei, supported by Hayashi Tatsuo sensei, in London for a weekend seminar; they also brought two nanadan sensei with them, Nishioka and Suzuki sensei, the latter being one of the few female 7th dans to have visited the UK. What made the seminar special for many of the attendees was that Hayashi sensei is American educated and acts as an official interpreter to the IKF, so translation was accurate and fluent.

As always on these occasions, the local 6th and 7th dans are asked to check that partipants are doing things correctly and getting the most from the drills, so I diligently listened to both Iwatate sensei's words and Hayashi sensei's translation. What struck me from the outset was that different teachers have very different approaches to the same end outcome. Our last UK seminar was with Chiba sensei, who advocates small cuts and a parallel style of striking dou for beginners up. Iwatate sensei is an evangelist for a big cutting motion, practised with the shinai touching your bottom on the backswing, even for dou.

The logic is irrefutable. By cutting in this way, you learn to use your shoulder joints in a relaxed manner. As the seminar progressed, sensei explained and demonstrated that as you progressed up the grading ladder, your attacks could then become smaller whilst retaining the suppleness gained from big movements. Another impressive element was the way that, throughout the drills, sensei managed to incorporate and build upon the elements of kikai and seme.

So, an excellent seminar which, I am sure, did a lot to improve the kendo of most of the people there. I, however, was most impressed by Iwatate sensei's closing words in which, almost as if he read my mind, he explained that in a lifetime's kendo we all get varied information and instruction from a variety of teachers. In his words, the trick is to judge in your own mind which of these approaches and techniques is right for you and to build on them accordingly. To sum up in my words, there are some great teachers out there, but only you can make your kendo work for you.

24

Enzan no metsuke

The sequence of perception to waza in kendo is described as ichi gan, ni soku, san tan, shi riki.

- One – (gan) sight
- Two – (soku) feet
- Three – (tan) abdomen (centre / courage)
- Four – (riki) power (technique)

In my understanding, we see the opportunity, immediately push off from the back foot, committing the whole of our power from tanden, and complete the technique when we reach the target.

Notwithstanding tales of Zatoichi (the blind swordsman), sight is the first element of any kendo technique and the way that we watch our opponent is crucial to the success of our attack. If we stare at the target we are going to strike, we give our opponent obvious notice of our intention. If we look just at his or her face to try to understand their next action, we may miss the signals they give when they start to move hands or feet. If we look just at feet or hands, we can be easily tricked by movement designed to get our attention. If we look at the point of the shinai, there is even more chance that we may be fooled by a feint. We therefore use enzan no metsuke, (the way of looking at a far mountain).

As the name suggests, enzan no metsuke is a way of looking at the whole picture: the overall shape of your opponent, his body, hands, feet, shinai and face, particularly his eyes.

At first you may need to train yourself to do this. Hopefully, with experience, it becomes second nature. Enzan no metsuke requires a clear unfettered mind, sometimes referred to as heijoshin (normal mind). You should not anticipate or second guess your opponent's action, but instead your mind should be a mirror that reflects his true actions and intentions, allowing you to act instantly.

No matter how perfect your perception becomes, it is of little value unless you can develop technique that flows equally instinctively; you can only do this through regular, concentrated keiko.

25

Sports kendo versus shugyo

I was gratified by the high level of feedback to the article on "The Aim of Kendo" by Matsumoto sensei. I know that many of the people who commented are active shiai participants. This bolstered my view that an understanding of kendo philosophy is a natural bedfellow for hard training and ambition to do well in shiai.

Some time ago, when I was making one of my uncharitable online rants against Iai, I received a good natured comment giving an Iaidoka's view of the respective questions likely to be asked by followers of either art:

Iai keiko – "Did I manage to cut kasso teki; did I incorporate kankyukyojaku when attacking; did I exhibit fukaku throughout my embu?"

Kendo keiko – "Did I go commando today?"

I certainly take his point, but to be honest I would assume that, in the true spirit of zen martial arts, you either exhibited kankyukyojaku and fukaku or you didn't and, in

the same way, you either went commando or you didn't –
and if you didn't you should be ashamed of yourself.

The point I am trying to get to is that, as Matsumoto
sensei said, "It is the true aim of kendo practice not only
to try to improve your technique, but also to train your
mind and spirit to find the rightness of mind ("no mind"
/ mushin), so that your mind, which is the source of the
technique, will not be bound by anything." So, in short,
we should train without being overtly analytical, but
should reflect on how we achieve correct kendo attitude.

So where does shiai fit in? Surely it is the opportunity to
test how you have progressed, both in the development
of technique and the strength of your mental attitude in
as close a situation to "real" shinken kendo as can legally
be engaged in. When you are under pressure in shiai, this
is the time when the conscious mind shuts down and the
reflexes gained through hard training take over.

Some dojo will tell you, "We do not teach shiai kendo. Our
approach is based upon traditional kendo." This seems to
me to be based on slightly strange reasoning as kendo
developed as a means to settle "life or death" contests.

I have a view that what these "traditionalists" are really against is the use of cheap tricks to win in shiai. This is a sentiment with which I wholeheartedly agree, but I also believe that in high level shiai it is the kendoka who have invested thousands of hours of grueling basic practice and who avidly read about the experiences and philosophy of previous generations of sensei, who triumph in the shiaijo.

26

Dou – collective hanshi wisdom!

Many people who can confidently hit men and kote continue to have difficulty with dou. This is not surprising as, whilst men and kote are obvious targets that only require you to raise and lower the shinai in a straight line, dou is harder to see and hit.

There is some confusion over what part of the dou constitutes the target. The right side is the correct striking area and the front "hara dou" is not counted as a valid strike. The main reason for dou to fail, however, is because of poor posture or because hasuji is incorrect when contact is made.

Having recently been shown dou by both Chiba sensei and Sumi sensei, I was relieved to see that even though their kendo styles and approach to teaching are very different, the key point on dou-uchi made by them both is absolutely consistent. "Your right hand must be pushed forward so that it is directly in front of you at the point of impact." This is regardless of which timing and opportunity the attack takes and the direction of your footwork.

If we look at the chances to strike dou, we can occasionally make a successful shikake dou attack; this could be as a debana or hikibana technique when your opponent starts to lift his arms to hit men, or as a hikiwaza if he pushes his hands up to counter your downward pressure in tsubazeriai.

Dou, however, is more likely to be successful as an oji waza, either as nuki or kaeshi dou against a men attack. With nuki-dou, you move your body diagonally to the right to avoid your opponent's strike whilst at the same time hitting his dou. In this case, it is crucial to push your right hand straight forward as you hit, even though your body is moving away from the centre. If you do not do this, you will have to drop your hands and shoulders as you cut across the front of the dou. This will make you lean over to the side and force you to cut down diagonally with bent arms, achieving no power behind the cut.

For kaeshi dou against men, you need to block and return the attack in "the timing of one", whilst directly in front of the target. Only after making the strike should you start to move through to your right. One of the points that Sumi sensei makes is that it is also perfectly acceptable to move through to your left (opponent's right), to take zanshin for kaeshi dou.

Chiba sensei's unique spin on dou-uchi is that the path of your cut should be parallel with the floor, so that you strike with the bottom take of the shinai.

Whether your preference is for kaeshi or nuki dou, if you move through to the right you need to either release your left hand or slide it up the tsuka as you move through. You should also keep your eyes on your opponent until you have finished the attack.

27

Humility

The AJKF states that, "The concept of Kendo is to discipline the human character through the application of the principles of the katana." One of the virtues that we aim for in this process is humility. This is not easy to attain as success and growth in kendo calls for confidence and self-belief and, in the eyes of many people, these qualities do not sit easily with modesty.

Through blogs like this and through comments on social media, it is easy to instantly express feelings about our kendo. I often read posts from friends returning from a good practice that read along the lines of: "I was on fire", "I aced it", "I smashed it" etc. I know from personal experience that when keiko goes well, particularly if you have just "broken through the wall" after a period of frustration, you want to tell the world, but I am still not sure how to do it without sounding boastful.

Blowing your own trumpet is worse when it is done by more experienced kenshi. If after 30 or 40 years of "shugyo" we are still showing obvious basic character flaws, something is not working. Last year at the Kyoto Taikai, I was asked by a senior sensei what I thought of my performance after losing my tachiai, I stupidly mentioned that I was satisfied with my performance. I meant that I had tried my hardest, but having phrased it the way I did, I realised immediately how conceited it sounded.

There is a Japanese proverb that says, *"Minoru hodo kobe no sagaru inaho ka na"* 実るほど頭のさがる稲穂かな – "The bough that bears most *(fruit)* hangs lowest". This seems to be illustrated continuously by the really great kendo players, who let their actions speak for themselves. *Kenkyo* (modesty or humility) is of course central to Japanese culture, so people from countries where more direct communication is the norm may be forgiven the odd inadvertent boast. Nevertheless, kendo values come from Buddhist / Confucian roots where humility and obedience are prized.

Like most things, humility can be overstated. There are certainly cases where false modesty can be as annoying as boastfulness. "Oh no, I am only a beginner" sounds a bit trite after you have just won a major international Taikai.

Modesty is, of course, not just a Japanese trait. In the paraphrased words of Rudyard Kipling's poem "If": "If you can meet with Triumph and Disaster, And treat those two impostors just the same: you'll be a Man, my son!"

28

Ippon

Following the 15WKC referees' seminar in Japan and the Paris Taikai, and in preparation for the WKC, I am in the process of crystallising my thoughts on what is and what isn't ippon.

As with any other element of high level kendo, be it scoring the point yourself or validating the successful strike made by another, a large amount of "mushin" is involved. Whilst there are clear objective criteria for what makes a point, the action happens at a speed where an instantaneous, subjective reaction is required from the referees. The only question that there is time to answer is – Is it ippon?

Of course, the elements required to make a point are documented in the rule book. To achieve ippon a player must have the intention to hit the point. He must strike the correct target area with full spirit and correct posture, the strike must have *sae* or snap and zanshin must be shown after the attack. From a referee's perspective these points are law; however, in the time it takes an athlete to reach the target, the referee has no time to go through the check-list. He must make an instant decision.

A referee's evolution is similar to a child's. He starts copying Mum and Dad and his flags dutifully go up with those of the other referees. He then moves into the rebellious teenage period, where his decisions are most likely the opposite of his two peers. Finally, on maturity, he aims to harmonise with his team mates, (but not at the expense of truth as he sees it).

With experience, he learns to move so that he is better situated to see the competitors' movements and the reactions of his colleagues, even to anticipate the players' actions. Nevertheless, when an attack is made an instant decision is required, and it is what fills your eyes and ears at the time that dictates whether the flag is raised.

With that in mind, waza needs to be sharp, accurate and delivered with purpose. Zanshin should be full of spirit without celebration, otherwise you risk withdrawal of the point with torikeshi. Above all, ippon should be delivered with 100 percent commitment. If the player does not believe in his actions, it is unlikely that he can convince the referees to do so.

So, referees and shiaisha gambatte.

29

Wasabi

Sometimes, when talking to newer kendoka about the objectives and culture of kendo, I am reminded of a manzai comedy sketch I saw many years ago. The principal comedian asked a supposedly non-Japanese sidekick about his understanding of wabi sabi (the Japanese aesthetic of imperfection and oneness with nature). The foreign straight-man replied that he loved wasabi (Japanese green mustard) and how well it went with sushi and noodles.

The fact that we very seldom "get it" from day one, is not surprising! Kendo, whilst a sport, is built on a multi-layered philosophy incorporating Shinto and Confucian and Taoist thought, augmented by the principles of Zen. The difficulty in fully understanding the ethos of kendo is not reserved for beginners. Kendo's culture is similar in some ways to my Microsoft Office software. Most of us get really good use from about 30 percent of its functionality and seldom bother with the other 70 percent.

Motivations for taking up kendo are varied: from a love of *Star Wars* or Manga to an interest in Zen, or the fact that it simply "looked cool". For some people of Japanese heritage outside Japan, it's a link with their roots. In Japan the reasons are equally diverse: "Mum made me do it", "It was compulsory in school", "It was a way to get fit after the kids graduated from university" etc. Kendo, however, has a way of drawing in its practitioners, so that once in the routine of regular training it is hard to stop. The reasons for keeping going, if even thought about, are very different from the reasons for starting in the first place.

When I started kendo in Japan in the 1970s, most of my peers had continued on a path that started in the school system and had given little conscious thought to their reasons for training. Some of the senior members and teachers had started kendo before the Second World War and had been through the Occupation and the resultant ban on martial arts. I imagine that this hiatus had caused them to seriously reflect on their motivation before restarting practice. At the time, I did not have the temerity to ask directly about their experiences and the few conversations I had with them on the subject at drinking parties were hard to remember afterwards.

With hindsight, I wish that I had asked more questions, although I doubt that I would have received any more answers. The ethos at the time was that it would have been beyond impertinence for a beginner in their 20s to ask for justification from a master in their 70s. The response to philosophical questions was expressed physically. The treatment that I received, however, was always concerned and courteous. I imagine that, at the time, there must have been some internal debate between curiosity as to why a foreigner was interested in something so intrinsically Japanese, and the desire to evangelise the values of kendo.

I have reached the conclusion that whatever your ethnic background, the most important thing is starting kendo in the first place. Of course, the drop-out rate is enormously high. 90 percent of those who start kendo beginners' classes give up within six months. But for those who stick with it, the process of regular keiko does more to clarify the meaning of kendo than could any reading matter. The ZNKR *Purpose and Principles of kendo* is a good reference to kendo's values, but to quote Nike's advertising gurus, the best way to achieve knowledge is "Just do it".

Chakuso for shinpan or "A tale of two buttons"

I got a new blazer as a Christmas present, shortly after hearing of my selection as a referee for the 15WKC. I had lost a little weight since buying my last blazer, so decided on one with a smart tailored fit. I decided to break it in before the event and wore it to the Paris Taikai.

Feeling that I was looking as sharp as any kendo shinpan can look, I took my place in the sports hall some 30 minutes before the beginning of the event and thought that whilst the competitors were warming up, I should do a few stretches of my own. I started by throwing my arms out to loosen my shoulders and the top button of my two-button blazer took off.

Fortunately, I had some time before the first shiai, so I persuaded the nearby bogu seller to sew the offending button back in place. I then moved to my court for the first match. All went to plan for the first few contests, but later, as I took my position as shushin, disaster struck. As one of the competitors exited the shiaijo, I raised both flags to call yame; as I did so, the top button again took flight and hit the timekeeper. Fortunately he was using a whistle rather than a bell, otherwise it might have been the first and only example of a shushin calling yame and ringing "time" simultaneously.

Working on the premise that the best way to continue was with the minimum of fuss, I fastened the remaining bottom button before awarding hansoku and restarted the match. Within a few seconds, red scored a decisive men ari and I and my two colleagues raised our flags for ippon. As my flag went up I felt a draught against my shirtfront. The shushin in the next court stopped his match, picked up my second button and returned it to me. Now, of my two buttons, one was on the timekeeper's desk and the other in my inside pocket. Fortunately, red scored again and as this was the taisho match, the replacement referee team took over.

After a hurried group rei, I collected my remaining button and considered ways of getting through the day without looking a total slob. Luckily the emergency services were on hand. The Paris Ambulance Service very kindly went through their medical kit and found me two big safety pins which held my buttons in place for the rest of the day.

I have now reverted to "Plan D". On returning home I went to the sewing supplies shop and bough a reel of elastic thread. After making a total mess of sewing on the buttons, I enlisted my wife's help and now have the springiest blazer buttons in kendo. I will, of course, take my blazer for another test drive; otherwise it is back to the old model for the 15WKC.

31

Kendo and team sports

Anyone who lives in the UK is subjected to regular Monday morning conversations about football (or soccer to my North American friends). My own knowledge of "the beautiful game" is somewhat sketchy, having avoided playing throughout my school career. I do, however, accept that many people are passionate about the sport. Wherever possible, I resist the temptation when told that "We" won three nil, to ask, "What, apart from eating pies at the ground, or watching with a cold pint on the big screen at the pub, what was your contribution to the result?"

I am, though, becoming more exposed to football, although in a less than obvious way. There is a sports field complex at the bottom of my garden, so recently, whilst digging out the vegetable beds, I have been witness to a number of junior games. The conifers screen out a lot of the vision, but I certainly get the full audio experience. I have the (perhaps misguided) impression that for every player on the field there are two people needed to shout conflicting instructions. On Saturday, a young man called Curly seemed to be the centre of attention, with people simultaneously shouting, "Go forward, Curly", "Go back, Curly", "Get the ball, Curly" and "Get rid of it, Curly". All of these commands may have been relevant, but they resulted in poor Curly, who could not have been much older than seven, running on the spot and crying.

I, of course, made my normal comparison to kendo and realised that no matter how hard we coached Curly before the event, once in the shiai jo he would be master of his own destiny. The other obvious difference is that although he might be representing the honour of his dojo or his school, he would do so as an individual.

32

Brake and Accelerator

I was asked to suggest a theme for this weekend's Watchet seminar and I decided on braking and acceleration. No, I have not started giving driving lessons, but based on observation of high quality keiko compared with the kendo of less experienced kenshi, I am convinced that what sets the two apart is the ability explode into action from a standing start and to stop in a similarly short interval.

Shiai are won in the blink of an eye. As soon as an opportunity is created, we need to push off and hit in the timing of one. Once we have achieved ippon, we need to stop our forward movement and assume correct zanshin equally instantly. For many people in the early stages of their kendo career, the pattern of their attack is along the lines of – lift the shinai, step forward, hit and run through, building momentum only after the strike. Most people have heard the expression ichi-byoshi; this means to lift and hit in one smooth motion. The ability to achieve this relies not only on correct footwork and posture, but also on accurate breath control.

The ideal sequence is to take a deep breath whilst still in safe distance, release some of it as kakegoe whilst retaining the remainder in your abdomen as you step into you own preferred striking distance. Only when you see the opportunity to attack should you expel the rest of your breath by way of kiai as you strike the target. Your furikaburi and strike should be in one smooth motion as you push off from the left foot and make fumikomi with your right, smartly bringing up your left foot in hikitsuke. In the case of a men attack, where your opponent obliges by stepping aside after you hit, the explosion of your waza should allow you to smartly move through to a safe distance to turn and assume zanshin.

With kote or tsuki this is not always possible; you need to stop in front of your opponent in a strong kamae, without "running on" and potentially putting him or her in danger. This is where the brake comes into play. Stopping when you are in full spirit depends on good balance and posture. You need to ensure that your weight is between your feet and that you have a straight back and a low centre of balance. If you lean forward you will lose all control.

Get these two elements right and you move from being the kendo equivalent of a three-wheeler van to shaping up like a sparkling new Lamborghini.

33

15WKC Referees' decisions

The 15WKC is over. Kendo people from around the world are arriving home and sharing their impressions of the event with friends in their home countries. Athletes, coaches and supporters are still buzzing with euphoria or nursing their disappointment and starting to think about doing as well or better in Tokyo in 2015.

After my first WKC as a referee, I came away with mixed feelings of exhaustion, relief that I have so far not been featured on the referee mistakes videos on YouTube and surprise that I got home with all my possessions and none of my room-mate's after packing for the early morning airport bus just hours after the sayonara party.

For the referees it was a long week. We started with a referee seminar on Wednesday to reinforce the work we did in Japan in February, and then spent three long days in the arena. On Saturday we arrived at 8.00 in the morning and got back to our nearby hotel at 9.00 at night. The activity was constant; I may be a candidate for the World Speed Eating Prize, having demolished a four-course Italian lunch in a five-minute break.

The referee team inhabited a parallel universe for the course of the championship. We were either in the shiai-jo or segregated in our own hotel and, other than briefly socialising with each other over dinner and breakfast, did nothing apart from referee and sleep. Even amongst ourselves, there was no discussion on the accuracy of decisions made on court. At the two seminars prior to the competition, yuko datotsu were dissected in detail, but at the event, real time decisions are made in seconds, are incontestable and further debate is irrelevant.

I worked on Court A with a group of Korean, Japanese, Taiwanese, American and European colleagues. When we were sitting in the queue we stole the occasional glance at the performances of our own countries' teams, but, by and large, remained emotionally detached. When on court, everyone made their own series of split-second decisions with sincerity and without bias. My overall impression is that everyone gave their all and that the calls made in the centre of the arena under the scrutiny of the audience and the world's media were made to the best of our ability.

It is easy to make judgments when you are nursing a cold drink in the back row of the stands, but slightly tougher when you are in the spotlight. There have been debates about electronic bogu and video evidence to decide ippon. When you take into account the elements of distance, posture, intention, sae, hasuji, attacking spirit and zanshin that are integral to yuko datotsu, there seems to be little alternative to the current system, human error included.

34

Keiko with seniors

Now with the excitement of the 15 WKC behind us, I have returned to the routine of keiko in my regular dojo. Unfortunately, until Sueno sensei arrives in two weeks' time, I am back on the motodachi side.

As the saying goes, it is better to give than to receive. I very much enjoy practising with senior kendoka, be they more experienced nanadan, or better still, hachidan sensei. Having spent much of my kendo life on the junior side of the dojo, I am comfortable with my obligation as kakarite. In short, I know that I need to constantly attack any target that I see, be it hard fought for or gratuitously given to me. The old kendo adage, "see it, hit it" is crucial to being a good student.

If you see sensei's men you should strike with 100 percent of your energy in the feeling of sutemi (throwing away the seeds). If he takes away your opportunity and returns your strike with kaeshi dou it doesn't matter. The point is that you saw the chance and made a concerted, sincere attack.

Most kendoka understand this, but there are a few who, regardless of opponent, treat every keiko like a shiai, where not losing points is more important than making them. This attitude encourages blocking the opponent's technique with the shinai without the intention to counter. More bizarrely, I see people who drop their elbows to their sides to avoid having their dou hit. Perhaps the worst habit engendered by this approach is that of always holding back. By this I mean starting an attack but being prepared to stop it mid flow if the receiver tries a counter technique.

I believe that training in this way does not allow anyone's kendo to develop. Unless we are able to attack wholeheartedly when we see an opportunity, we will never achieve the holy grail of mushin. As for motodachi, he or she is there to help you. In hikitate-geiko, which is by and large the most common form of keiko between senior and junior, the objective is for motodachi to stay just slightly ahead of kakarite.

After fighting for shodachi, or first point, the teacher will normally create a number of subtle opportunities for his opponent to attack. This can be particularly useful if these openings stimulate techniques that kakarite do not normally use. For instance, if he or she tends to rely on counter techniques, then stepping back as you create an opening will encourage the use of hikibana waza and a more forward going approach.

Of course, motodachi deserves some fun from the process, so a positive, fearless kakarite who is not constantly worrying about being countered, allows him or her the chance to crack in the odd kaeshi dou or suriage men. Above all, both partners should remember that the purpose of keiko is for all of us to grow and develop.

35

The importance of suburi

Sueno sensei, hanshi hachidan and 1979 All Japan Championship winner from Kagoshima, is currently in the UK and has just given us a very interesting seminar. At the opening stage, he stressed the importance of continuing suburi throughout your kendo career and made the point that "If you can't do suburi, no matter how long your kendo experience, you can't do kendo."

He instructed that the path of the shinai in suburi should be smooth, in line with the centre of the body and close to the head, and that we should use all three joints: shoulders, elbows and wrists. He also insisted that we should ensure that we use the muscles in the underside of our arms rather than those on top. To achieve this, we should pull our arms back past the midpoint of the top of our heads and feel these muscles engage before starting the downswing. Once this has been achieved and the muscle memory kicks in, we are able to make our upswing smaller and smaller; in keiko or shiai, the cut can be as small as you wish as long as it has impact.. We should not pull our elbows out and arms should remain relaxed. When viewed from the back, our shoulder width should not change throughout the whole striking process.

Sueno sensei also talked about the old, commonly taught concept of shibori (wringing the hands on completion of the cut) being incorrect and that we should not change our grip from beginning to end of the cut. He explained that the hands throughout the cut should be in kirite (cutting hand) position, although they could be extended in nobite (extended hand) form to lengthen our reach on impact. He also torpedoed the old myth that we should straighten our right arm on cutting men by demonstrating that doing this gave a four to five centimetre reach advantage, but that the resultant body imbalance caused us to lose 30 or 40 centimetres of distance from our footwork.

Sensei then went on to take us through a sequence of waza geiko, uchikomi geiko and kakarigeiko exercises, constantly reinforcing the concept of accurate relaxed swing. The other key point that was accentuated was correct breathing. When you breathe in, you are open to attack so, before you enter fighting distance, you should breathe in quickly and conserve your breath in your tanden until you can conclude a successful waza. Finally, he made the point that if you miss with your attack you should keep going until you make a successful strike.

Although I was there in an assistant instructor role, the temptation to try things myself was overwhelming. The highlight of the seminar for me was a keiko with Sueno sensei, who was, of course, impossible to hit. As the old song goes, "It don't mean a thing, If you ain't got that swing".

36

Kote simplified

During his recent UK seminar, Sueno sensei made the point that "kote attack should be in a straight line". Sumi sensei backed this up during his visit last week, and Chiba sensei has certainly said more or less the same thing. So why, when we get back to our normal hanshi free keiko, do people revert to hitting kote from a variety of odd angles?

Beginners in particular tend to stand directly in front of their opponent and move the tip of the shinai to their left to attack kote. This has the effect of diagonally cutting across the soft tsutsu part of the kote rather than making a correct hit on the kote buton. The other common mistake is to rotate the shinai under the kote which leaves the left hand too low to make a correct strike.

The key point to bear in mind is that when we talk about cutting direct from our centre to the target, it does not mean the centre of our body should be directly in line with the centre of our opponent's body. It means that the centre of our body should be in a straight line with the target we are striking, be it men, do, or kote.

A useful tip for striking kote is to move your right foot over as you make the kote attack so that it lines up with your opponent's right foot, rather than his left, which would be the correct position from which to strike men. By doing this, your body is facing the target, although you are now positioned slightly to the left of your opponent. Your shinai should be in a straight line from your left hand, which should be in front of your navel, to your partner's kote.

Another thing to remember is that when you move from the centre to hit kote, you only have to move above the height of your opponent's shinai tip and no more than the width of his shinai to the left.

With this in mind, it is tempting to leave your left hand in place and just use right hand power to make the attack. This is wrong! Your left hand should do the bulk of the work and the right hand just keeps it on course and squeezes gently with equal pressure to the left hand to make tennouchi on impact.

A final caution! You only need to cut through the thickness of your partner's wrist. So the force of the attack should be forward. As Sumi sensei once eloquently put it, "like a chameleon's tongue coming out to catch a fly".

Kendo equipment and child labour

I have been asked for advice on a number of occasions about the best way to wash hakama and keikogi. If you wash them too often they lose colour; if you don't wash them often enough they become smelly and crusty. Putting both kendogi and bogu out to dry in the sunshine has a deodorising effect, but as we have had so little summer sun in the UK this year, washing has become a necessity.

Kendo clothing should ideally be washed by hand in cold water without soap powder, so to do this to best effect, and to find my grandson a useful occupation in the school holidays, I have developed the "Small Boy Kendo Washing Machine" or "Shonen Kendo Sentakuki". The key components are a small boy, a bucket and a hosepipe.

To avoid blue dye in the house and the resultant discussions with non-kendoka partners or housemates, the garments to be washed, the boy, bucket and hosepipe should be taken somewhere in the garden where they can be hung out to dry (the keikogi, that is, not the boy).

The keikogi and boy are placed in the bucket and he is given the hosepipe and instructions to half fill the bucket whilst jogging on the spot, and to keep going for 20 minutes and a number of water changes. He may need some help on this one and have to be lifted out at each water change.

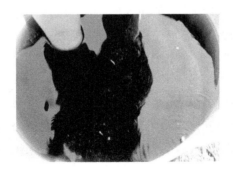

Once the boy has done his bit, you need to ensure that you rinse the blue dye off his feet before you hand him back. To dry hakama, it is best to use a clip-type hanger and turn the koshiita down in line with the front waistband. You can then pull the pleats in place before it dries, minimizing or avoiding the need for ironing. Keikogi should be turned inside out and dried on a pole that passes through both sleeves. Special keikogi hangers that extend to the correct shape are available from most budo stores. My favourite method is to take a slat from a carbon fibre shinai, drill two holes in the centre and attach a hook through a string. Come to think of it this is, to my mind, the best use of a carbon fibre shinai.

I am sure that these revelations will cause concern amongst right thinking people who shun the exploitation of minors, but rest assured I make the task less intimidating with a plentiful supply of ice lollies, Jaffa Cakes and Fizzy Fangs.

38

"Boys be ambitious"

I am no longer surprised by beginners who, after a few weeks in armour, are bursting to take up nito or jodan. Everyone who starts kendo does so with a vision of the kenshi that they wish to become. Of course, having a goal to aim for is totally worthy. William S. Clark's parting words to the students of Sapporo Agricultural College, "Boys be ambitious", became common currency in Japan, and are still quoted 130 years after he said them.

We live in an instant age. Whereas singers and musicians used to achieve fame after years of learning their trade by gigging in pubs and clubs, today's "superstars" reach their dreams by appearing on talent shows. Clearly this view is slightly coloured by my status as a "grumpy old man", but as a member of the "me" generation, I am probably as much to blame as is Simon Cowell. To face facts, there are no instant gains in kendo. Skill is built on years of hard training.

I have discussed the challenges of building patience into the kendo learning process with a number of my betters, particularly Chiba sensei. His view as a jodan player is that until you can invariably produce accurate waza from chudan with correct ki-ken-tai-itchi, you should not move on to the more esoteric aspects of kendo. If you can't control one sword then you are doubling the difficulty with two, and if your feet and hands don't work together you will not solve the problem by reversing your foot position when you take jodan. In my humble (and Chiba sensei's less humble) view, good kendo is built on the foundation of following good instruction and repeatedly practising basic techniques in chudan.

The stage at which people should embark on a shiai career follows similar logic. It is admirable to want to test your skill in competition against others, but unless you can do basic techniques correctly, you risk developing bad habits that could spoil your further development. One or two early exposures to competition will probably help confirm your place in the kendo universe, but without a good basis of accurate fundamental kendo, continued training with shiai in mind will harm rather than help your future development.

So far it all sounds rather gloomy, but to my mind, the joy in learning kendo is in training for its own sake and when something falls into place then the pleasure of achievement is enormous. Of course, when you have assembled your kendo toolkit you can go on to become a great shiai player, whether in chudan, jodan or nito. As good old Bill Clark might have said, "Boys be ambitious, but give it a bit of time".

39

Sutemi and shishin

Most kendoka have heard the term "sutemi". Whilst usually translated as sacrifice, the literal meaning is "throw away the seed". The concept refers to a poem describing a horse chestnut in a fast moving stream. If left whole, it would sink. If the kernel is abandoned, the husk would float with the current. In kendo, sutemi means committing yourself one hundred percent to an attack without fearing the consequences.

Shishin, on the other hand, is the state where the mind is preoccupied with, or dwells on a particular aspect of, your or your opponent's kendo, which makes it impossible for the body to move freely. No prizes for guessing that sutemi is regarded as a desirable element in kendo and shishin is not.

Correct tobikomi men is a practical illustration of sutemi. We enter our opponent's distance and launch ourselves forward with full spirit and no thought other than hitting men. If our opponent moves away or counters, it doesn't matter. Once you start a technique you should complete it with all your energy.

In uchikomi-geiko or kakari-geiko it is easy to take this do or die attitude; in shiai or jigeiko it is more difficult. Very often we worry about our opponent's reaction to our attack. For some people this causes a general fear of attacking. For others, it results in them stopping mid-technique rather than giving away the point. This "stopping" is my pet hate in keiko. Not only does it strangle many potentially successful shikake waza at birth, but it also robs the stopper's opponent of the opportunity to practise oji-waza.

Many people take the view that shiai is about not losing, but surely the reason for taking part is to win. It could be argued that both equate to the same thing, but the mindset of winning is about courageously exploiting any opportunity with all your mental and physical power.

In keiko we talk about utte-hansei, utarete-kansya (reflection on how we made a successful strike and gratitude for being hit). This does not mean that we are masochists, but that we learn as much from our opponent's success as we do from our own.

Of course, we do not start any keiko with the intention of being hit. Our objective is to strike first or to break our opponent's attack with a successful counter attack, but we can only do this if we have an attacking spirit from the outset.

40

Sae

I am back from a weekend of kendo. On Saturday I ran a coaching session for the British Kendo Squad and on Sunday I refereed The British Open Championships. It was an interesting combination of events as the second day allowed everyone to work on putting theory into practice.

I have written about sae on a number of occasions. This term describes the snap or sharpness necessary to turn a strike into a successful yuko datotsu. This and seme were the themes of the squad training session. Whilst we looked at a number of shikake and oji techniques, we paid particular attention to both how we made the opportunity for and how we finished each attack.

Sae, in theory, is a product of tenouchi, (the inside of the hands), or the way you complete the cut by squeezing the tsuka of the shinai as it makes contract with the target. In practice, the path of the cut also has to be correct and ki-ken-tai-itchi has to bring all the elements of footwork, posture and kiai together at the exact point of striking the target. Sae is not something than can be applied as an afterthought. If your hands are in the correct position throughout the strike then it is simply a matter of squeezing with the little and ring fingers of both hands on the point of impact. If they are not and, for instance, your right hand is holding too strongly, then regardless of whether or not you squeeze the shinai, it will not result in ippon.

Chiba sensei talks about making tenouchi for men once the shinai is at chin height. The concept is to hit the target and then squeeze after, so that you strike with full force and complete the technique sharply just below the point of impact. This is not as aggressive as it sounds, because if the use of shoulders, elbows and wrists are correct, the strike will be quick and sharp rather than heavy.

At yesterday's taikai we saw varying levels of sae. There were many long encho where both fighters made numerous strikes, but few were sharp enough to make the referees raise their flags. At the end of the day we were presenting prizes and cleaning the hall at the same time. There was of course some enjoyable kendo. Mr Yamazaki, from Hokkaido University took first place, demonstrating my sae theory with some explosive techniques, including an excellent tsuki in the semi-final. I was also delighted that two of our regular Mumeishi students, Alex Heyworth and Alan Thompson, respectively took second and third place medals.

On a completely different subject, I had a Skype chat with a Japanese kendo friend who recently returned home after many years in the UK. He visited the Shudokan in Osaka and mentioned that he had to wait 45 minutes for keiko with a hachidan sensei. Nothing changes!

41

Waiting in line

I briefly mentioned in my last post that a friend who recently returned to Japan was surprised at having to wait for 45 minutes of a one-hour practice for keiko with a hachidan sensei in the Osaka Shudokan. George, who witnessed and commented on the scene, will, I am sure, back me up when I say this is not an unusual situation.

At the Shudokan, or any of the big civic dojo in Japan, you have to be quick and determined to practise with any of the senior sensei. The rule of thumb, when I was regularly training there, was that you could have two keiko with hachidan, four with nanadan, or up to eight at peer level in the allotted hour.

Getting face time with senior sensei is an acquired skill. You need to put your men on faster than any of your rivals and be prepared to run to position whilst pulling your kote on. Some kendoka train themselves to tie their men in record time, others develop ingenious ways to pre-tie their men so that it can be slipped on instantly.

These skills are equally useful for the monthly godokeiko sessions at the Nippon Budokan or asa-geiko at the Kyoto Taikai. Even though there may be 200+ hachidan in attendance, the chance of getting to your favourite hanshi is close to nil. On one occasion in Kyoto I made it my goal to be first in line with Sumi sensei. I got up at 4.30am, arrived almost an hour before practice started and placed myself approximately in front of the spot where he would be sitting. Fortunately for him, not so for me, he had been awarded hanshi the previous day so, whilst he initially sat facing the spot where I was waiting, he was pushed up the line by the longer time served, but still kyoshi sensei. I had to run an extra 20 metres to beat the queue and finished 5th in line. Nevertheless, I got my keiko.

Keiko with senior teachers offers two opportunities: one to practise with them and benefit from their advice; plus the chance to watch them with other students whilst you wait. The watching or mitorigeiko part becomes more interesting if sensei's opponents are other kodansha. The downside is that usually they have the right to queue jump. This is a sensible arrangement as it allows them to get back to acting as motodachi with a minimum of delay. If however you are last in line and there is five minutes of keiko time left and someone steps in front of you, you may not see it that way.

Returning to the challenges of making the most of your time in the dojo, the Japanese system for adult kendoka is essentially, well, adult. You can invest your time in waiting to train with the top teachers or, if you think it is needed, you can stay at the shimoseki end of the dojo and practise kihon geiko with a buddy of your own grade. As long as you take your keiko seriously, no-one will mind.

42

Tsubazeriai in top level kendo

I have just returned from the keiko after the Mumeishi 3s. This was a full-on two-and-a-half hour session with some 200 people in attendance. I was reminded that in my last post I underestimated the motodachi count by one 7th dan, but even with eight of us plus one 8th dan and numerous 6th dans it was still hard work.

The previous day's taikai went without a hitch and Mumeishi's "A" team won. This was a great way for the club to celebrate the event's 40th anniversary. My job was that of shinpan-shunin, running "A" Court under the direction of our shinpan-cho, Sumi sensei. The overall standard of shiai was excellent and the referees did a good job in keeping everything moving. My only complaints were in the few cases where overzealous referees stopped shiai too frequently for minor points. Sumi sensei did, however, let me know that we should have dealt more strictly with one case of tsubazeriai infringement. Of course when a hanshi tells you something like this, you answer "Yes" and make sure that it does not happen again.

Sumi sensei, however, is a very approachable hanshi and later at the after competition party we talked frankly about how strictly the tsubazeriai rules are enforced. I mentioned that I had attended the two World Championship referee seminars this year and the instructors had made it clear what was and what was not acceptable for tsubazeriai and what counted as a clean break on wakare. In effect, tsubazeri is only legal if the shinai are crossed at the tsuba on the omote side. The shinai should not touch your opponent and neither of you should touch your own or your partner's jinbu. On wakare both parties should break cleanly so that the shinai are clear of each other.

Nevertheless, at the World Championships numerous examples of the players either covering the shinai from the ura side, or attacking before making a clean break on command were allowed by highly experience referees.

Sumi sensei made the point that at this year's Asia zone referee seminar the most asked question was "Why should we penalise this behaviour when it is becoming normal practice at the All Japan Championship?" Quite a difficult point to answer, I imagine.

There is obviously a divergence between the theory of good kendo and the practicalities of not getting beaten, which needs to be resolved at the highest levels. In the meantime, we can start by encouraging good kendo by enforcing the rules in our local competitions.

43

Hidari de motsu!

I once spent an enlightening 30 or so minutes sitting in seiza listening to a post keiko lecture from Kaku sensei in Nara. Kaku sensei's theme was Hidari de motsu, hidari de utsu "You hold with your left (hand) and hit with your left". The driving force behind the lecture was that Kaku sensei had observed that many of the students at the practice were using too much right hand power and were therefore not striking effectively.

The extended seiza must have helped drive this lesson home, because it is easy to see that many of the problems of overextension, poor posture and inaccurate cutting are caused by the application of too much right hand power. The stiffness that we looked at in my last post is often "one sided" caused by the overuse of the right arm.

Many people overuse the right hand in an attempt to make small waza. The left hand becomes a fixed pivot and their cutting action is based on pulling the shinai back and pushing it forward with the right hand almost as if they were trying to touch their own nose with the shinai. Whilst this might appear to make the attack quicker, it typically has the opposite effect.

Correct cutting, whether large or small, relies on the left hand raising the shinai to a point where it can be brought down on the target. The right hand is very much the junior partner; it follows the left hand on its upward path and only makes a real contribution by squeezing to make tenouchi after the point of impact. In the case of men uchi, this means raising the left hand to a point above your own men gane and then striking down. The right arm should be relaxed and not over-straightened on the point of hitting. There should be a very slight flexion in your elbow and both shoulders should be square-on to the target.

With small techniques such as kote, the left hand should play its part, even if it is to lift the shinai no higher than the point of your opponent's shinai. In this case it is a matter of striking sharply forward rather than down, but it is the left hand that does most of the work.

The benefits of doing this are enormous. It allows you to stay relaxed and to keep your posture correct and remain square on to your opponent. When your posture is correct you can push more easily from the left foot, maintaining correct ki-ken-tai-itchi and the shinai is more likely to hit the correct part of the target with sharp sae. The added bonus is you use far less energy.

So whilst my knees complained at the time, I owe a vote of thanks to Kaku sensei for the lecture.

44

Aggressive ojiwaza

A comment on an old post on suriage men arrived yesterday. This, plus a session that I ran in the dojo this week on ojiwaza, invigorated my interest in exploring the subject a little more.

A professional educator friend told me never to tell people what not to do, but to accentuate the positive actions that they should be taking. Nevertheless, I am going to point out what does not work when making oji techniques:

- Bringing the point of the shinai back towards your body makes it impossible to achieve correct suriage or kaeshi waza

- Dropping the point of your shinai, unless for ukenagashi (which we almost never use in shinai kendo), is a no-no

- Blocking and cutting in two separate actions also dooms you to failure

- It is nearly impossible to make suriage waza against overly large, badly-timed or off-centre cuts

- Waiting for your opponent to attack before you react is a waste of time

At the risk of confusing readers, one of the biggest problems we encounter in ojiwaza practice drills is in starting your counter attack before the opponent starts his strike. Because it is a drill we obviously know what is coming, so we are tempted to attack too early. I often see what should be suriage men turn into debana men.

Whilst I can think of so many don'ts, I can only think of three imperative "dos":

- Always push the point of the shinai forward when meeting your opponent's technique. This applies to all suriage and kaeshi waza

- Always make oji waza in "the timing of one" sliding up or blocking on the upstroke and cutting down to the target in the same movement, using just one step

- Always control the timing by inviting your opponent to attack

This last point applies equally to drills and to jigeiko and shiai. If from chudan you squeeze the shinai gently with the little finger of your right hand, your point will move towards his left eye. More often than not, this will make him attack your men at a time when your energy is focussed and you are able to respond immediately with suriage men or kaeshi dou. Move the shinai slightly to his right and he is likely to attack your kote, leaving you set up to make kote suriage men.

One effective way to practise oji waza was taught by Chiba sensei. The class forms groups of between five and nine. Everyone takes a turn as motodachi and the rest of the group are split into two smaller groups, one facing him and one behind. Each makes either a men or kote attack, either at random or the group in front attacks men and the group behind kote. Motodachi faces each in turn, turning from group to group and makes the appropriate oji technique, remembering to invite the attack in his or her own timing.

The key point is to control the timing of the attack by holding and breaking centre in the way described.

45

Encouraging beginners – or how to be a successful motodachi

My local dojo is looking at ways to help new kendoka make the transition from beginners' course to taking part in regular keiko sessions. To this end, I am running several motodachi training sessions for the more experienced members so they can help and encourage their newer colleagues.

Many people who start kendo do so through structured beginners' courses where they have the comfort of learning new skills as a group and where they are not expected to go one-on-one in competition with experienced players. After graduation from a brief period of learning basics, they are trussed up in unfamiliar bogu and left to take their chance in jigeiko, often with inexperienced motodachi, who are more concerned about improving their own technique than helping the newbie.

This invariably results in loss of confidence and adds to kendo's exceptionally high attrition rate. The kendo diary of many aspiring kenshi runs along the lines of: week 1 –

start beginners' course, week 6 – buy bogu, week 7 – decide not to go to dojo, week 8 – advertise bogu on eBay.

Thinking about the effort involved in starting such a challenging hobby as kendo, it seems a shame that we lose so many students through our own lack of empathy or knowledge of how to best develop them. Traditionally, in Japan, most kendoka started as children and there is a natural progression through the school system. Teaching adult beginners is a relatively new aspect of kendo, but it is particularly important in the west where people begin kendo at all ages.

For new kendoka, kihon drills in or out of bogu are not particularly threatening. It is when they begin to line up for motodachi geiko against their more experienced dojo mates that the experience can make or break them. One of the biggest problems is that most of us are not taught to be motodachi and we learn through trial and error. There are correct ways to receive kirikaeshi, uchikomi geiko and kakarigeiko and we need to learn these to get the best out of students. Most importantly, we need to learn that jigeiko is not a "one size fits all" activity and that we can break it down into gokakugeiko, which takes place between partners of equal level, and hikitategeiko, where a senior leads a junior.

Here are a few simple motodachi tips:

- For kirikaeshi, make sure that you receive the strikes close to your men. This way you encourage kakarite to attack the correct target.

- In uchikomigeiko, wait until kakarite enters the correct distance and try to build "mind pressure" before making the opening. If you show the target when he is out of distance he will develop the habit of running in, rather than learning to make one step, one cut.

- In kakarigeiko, keep a relaxed, soft chudan and allow kakarite to make his own opportunities.

- In hikitate geiko, try to keep only half a dan's difference in level between you. Keep your own seme and pressure and by all means go for the first ippon "shodachi", but encourage kakarite by allowing good strikes to connect.

Acting as motodachi is not just a one-sided act of charity, you can develop your own kendo whilst helping others.

46

Hikitategeiko

One of the benefits of writing this blog is that I get feedback from kendoka in other dojo and other countries about the way they do things and the challenges they face. This often stimulates ideas that I use when physically teaching kendo. Thomas Sluyter's comments on kirikaeshi following my last post helped me refine the drills for our group at Sanshukan.

One thing becoming obvious as we go through these sessions is that the theory is relatively easy to explain, but that it takes constant practice to develop motodachi skills. Hikitategeiko, in particular, is an area where experience is essential. No matter how well you understand the theory, unless you are able to read your opponent and build and relax the tension between you, it is unlikely that you will reach the desired outcome.

Just to reiterate, hikitategeiko is jigeiko between a senior and junior partner. Motodachi uses the opportunity to practise his own technique whilst encouraging kakarite to do his best. It works if the more experienced player sets the standard reasonably close to the junior's level, so that he acts as if he has only half a dan grade advantage.

By this, I do not mean that his technical kendo standard should be lowered, more that the competitive advantage is narrowed.

At the beginning of every keiko you should treat each opponent with the same level of respect. I therefore think that it is your duty to face him earnestly and to try for shodachi or the first point. You may be surprised that the junior player is the first to achieve this. No matter who takes the first ippon, this is a chance to study your opponent: how he moves, his strengths and weaknesses. You should continue to make your own opportunities, using seme, to penetrate his centre and maintain kizeme (mental pressure) to put him at a disadvantage. When, however, he makes a strong attack you should allow it to connect.

This is the ideal opportunity to practise your oji waza, so use hiki dasu to invite his strikes and then respond with suriage or kaeshi techniques. Do not, however, break his spirit by countering every attack. It goes without saying that you should not block, physically stop him with the point of your shinai, or resort to mis-timed or sneaky waza to make a point.

Depending on kakarite's level, there will come a point in the keiko when the tension between you breaks down. This is normally because his level of concentration and focus is starting to diminish. By now, you should have evaluated any bad habits or mistakes, so make the transition to uchikomigeiko, making opportunities for him to strike. Do this in a way where you use pressure to control distance and opportunity so that he strikes with correct timing and maai. Use this chance to make him correct any errors. You may have to demonstrate how to do the technique yourself, but do so quickly and keep conversation to a minimum. If it requires a long debate, have it in the pub after training.

If kakarite is relatively skilled, perhaps uchikomigeiko should be reduced to just one or two techniques at the end of the keiko. It may even be that you finish with ippon shobu, but if kakarite is that strong, we are moving into the realm of gokakugeiko.

47

Grading examinations for older kendoka

Reflecting on the Brussels grading, I am reminded that the higher your age, the more difficult it becomes to pass. In my experience, this is not just true for Europe, but applies everywhere including the kodansha grading examinations in Japan.

Now, I don't for a moment think that kendo is ageist. We are privileged to be able to participate at ages that would have exceeded the retirement points in many other sports. Nor, when looking at the array of venerable sensei on some grading panels, do I think there is any bias against senior candidates. It is, however, an irrefutable truth that it becomes more difficult to force your body to do good kendo as you reach your 50s and 60s.

Knees and ankles wear out, particularly after years of training on hard floors. Forward motion becomes more difficult and some older kenshi start to rely more on upper-body strength to hit the target. Unfortunately this is not the way forward.

I was fortunate to receive some concerted coaching from Chiba sensei when in my mid 50s that made me realise that I had to adapt my kendo to my age. The key points were that you needed to find your own distance, keep your footwork light but still forward, and use your opponent's movement to your advantage. Rather than making your attacks bigger and harder, they should be smaller and lighter.

The more you advance in grade, the more important seme becomes. This does not mean that you should constantly push in to take shikake waza, but you should also use hiki-dasu to make your opponent move towards you so that you can execute debana and oji-waza. The logic is that when your opponent steps towards you, you need only take half a step to reach the target. And it's not always necessary to make fumikomi. A sliding step forward can be sufficient if you have good ki-ken-tai-itchi. Zanshin is, of course, important, but you do not need to gallop across the dojo to make your point. Two or three steps through with good posture and kamae, before turning to re-engage, should be enough.

Kizeme is a necessity. Mochida sensei's often quoted truth that when your body becomes frail you have to rely on "indomitable spirit" to subdue your opponent, is key. You should use your mental strength to make the opponent move in a direction and timing where you can hit him. One of my other favourite quotes on this subject is from Kikuchi Koichi sensei, who said, "As I become older I move more slowly, but I also see my opponent's movement more slowly."

48

Difficult Dou

I returned last night from the French Open Championship in Paris where I was acting as a referee. This is a very big and popular taikai with individual and team matches held over two days. As well as competitors from all over France, I saw players from Sweden, Italy, the UK and from Japan.

Events like this are great opportunities to catch up with old friends, and in Paris there is the added bonus of good food and wine to finish each day.

From a referee's perspective, it is interesting to work in different environments with referees from other countries. Although of course, wherever you are, the basics of judging yuko-datotsu do not change.

Referees on my court were from France, Belgium, Japan and the UK. Over the two days we raised our flags for hundreds of men and kote and quite a few tsuki ari. We also saw numerous attempts at dou for which we gave only one ippon. Talking this over with my colleagues, the reasons for not awarding a point to most dou attacks is that they do not have correct hasuji, or they hit with the wrong part of the shinai.

As with men and kote, it is essential that the datotsu bu of the shinai strikes the correct part of the target. That is to say, the top third of the jinbu should hit the right side of the dou with the bottom take making contact. Most of the unsuccessful attempts we saw were "hira uchi", where the side of the shinai hits the dou. There were also a number of occasions where the front of the dou became the target. Normally this is not intentional but happens because the cut is made as the opponent is coming forward and there is not sufficient distance between you.

My pet theory as to why so few dou succeed is that most people view kaeshi dou or nuki dou as a reactive technique. If your opponent has already launched his attack and you attempt dou, you will be too close to complete the technique successfully. If, on the other hand, you force him to attack men and then hit dou just as he starts his attack, you should be able to hit the correct part of the dou with the right part of the shinai.

It helps to think about punching forward with your right hand while directly in front of your opponent and in turning your right wrist in so that the bottom take connects. Then you can move elegantly past your opponent and watch all three flags go up.

49

Apply tension and relax

One of our newer members is a professional musician. His kendo is visibly improving from week to week, but like almost everyone who starts as an adult he tends to use more physical power than he needs to.

Trying to find an easy analogy, I thought about my experience as an incompetent bedroom guitarist and realised that the inability to relax was the major reason for my lack of progress. When you watch great musicians they seem able to chill completely and just come in on the beat with lightest of touches. Amateurs like me, on the other hand, can be seen staring intently at the fret-board with their tongues poking out as they manfully prod at the strings.

In kendo, relaxation is equally if not more important. You have to relax in order to keep an effective kamae and to be able to move easily. Shoulders, elbows, wrists and your grip on the shinai must be loose and must remain so throughout the striking process. People are often confused by the instruction to apply pressure, or tension, and relax. What is generally meant is that your legs, hips and abdomen should be braced, but that your chest, shoulders and arms should not be tense.

To get this feeling you should push your shoulders back as if you are trying to make your chest feel wider. Then you should check that there is space between your upper arms and the sides of your body. Elbows should be bent. There is no reason why your left arm should not rest on your dou. Your right arm should certainly not be straight, as some people believe that it should, as it would pull your right shoulder forward and spoil your kamae.

Your left wrist needs to be turned slightly outwards to support the shinai, but this does not mean that it should be tense. Your right wrist should be in a completely natural position. Your grip should be relaxed. You need to grip only with the little and ring fingers of each hand, with the other fingers following without making intentional contact with the tsuka of the shinai. The points of contact for the gripping fingers are the finger tips and the opposing point of the palm. You should not apply pressure with the inside surface of the fingers. Finally, your tenouchi on striking the target should amount to no more than a squeeze without changing your grip.

Of course, with kendo and music and, I imagine, any other activity that requires physical dexterity, the more you practise the more relaxed you become. Maybe there is a chance that if I keep playing my scales I may become another Carlos Santana or Eric Clapton. At the current rate of progress it should only take another 120 years.

50

To push or not to push

To mix a number of metaphors... The road to kendo satori is paved with conflicting advice. We have to choose or, more likely, we are told either to put our tenugui inside or outside our men before or after practice, to make our suburi bigger or smaller and to use or not use tai-atari as part of kirikaeshi.

The kirikaeshi question is an interesting one. For such a standardised, widely practised exercise, there is considerable variation between the ways it is taught in different dojo. Distance, speed and timing tend to vary, there are two schools of thought as to where the break in continuous breathing should be, but the key point of contention is whether or not to make tai-atari after the shomen strike, before starting on the yoko-men sequence.

If you are a kendo student, the chances are that you will have no say in how you do the drill. The way you go about it will be dictated by your instructor's preference. Having said that, a thoughtful instructor will take your experience and skill level into account.

Tai-atari in kirikaeshi replicates the situation in keiko or shiai when the opponent remains in front of you after your first attack. You need to move into tsubazeriai and push him backward and attack again, either with a hikibana or hikiwaza technique. So it's a useful thing to practise. On the other hand, unless your posture is developed to a level where you can constantly keep your hips and centre engaged while relaxing your shoulders, making tai-atari immediately after a men attack causes you to lean forward and use your shoulders. This makes you unstable and therefore unable to move quickly to the next technique.

What I am trying to say in a rather long-winded way, is that if you can do tai-atari correctly, then do it. This means that your posture should be completely upright, but when you make contact with your opponents' hands you should lower your hips and push down lightly, not relying on upper body strength.

If, on the other hand, this is new to you, then the best way forward is not to push, but to remain in the position in which you hit men as your partner steps back into the correct distance for you to start the yoko-men sequence. In some dojo this is practised with an emphasis on motodachi creating as much distance as possible – to encourage kakarite to stretch to reach the target.

My personal view is that this no-touch approach will serve most people well up to 3rd dan level, but again, your instructor should know best.

51

Creating opportunities to strike

I have been asked to put some thoughts together on the theory of creating opportunities to strike in preparation for next weekend's Watchet seminar. With kendo being such a well-trodden path, this requires very little creativity from me; it's more a question of opening the kendo books on the correct page and reading what our predecessors had to say on the subject.

The whole spectrum of attacking opportunities in kendo is summed up in the Sansappo (or Sansatsuho) , which translates as "the three methods". These are:

- Ken wo korosu – kill the sword

- Waza wo korosu – kill the technique

- Ki wo korosu – kill the spirit

While these terms sound suitably esoteric, if you rearrange the order and group the techniques that represent these categories, you get a basic, common-sense list of which waza work in which circumstances.

- Ki wo korosu – equals seme. Using your whole body and, more importantly, your mental strength (kizeme), you push firmly into your opponent's space and destroy his mental composure, creating the opportunity to strike.

- Ken wo korosu – you break his kamae by moving his shinai with your own. Ways to do this include harai, osae, uchiotoshi and maki waza. Effectively, you sweep, push, knock down or twist his shinai away from his centre, leaving the door open for your attack.

- Waza wo korosu – this covers the whole range of oji waza. You make him attack and take the opportunity to destroy his technique and beat him with your own. To do this you can select from a menu of debana, suriage, kaeshi and nuki techniques. Which you use depends on how advanced his attack is before you strike. Debana waza is used when he starts his attack, suriage waza when his shinai is on its way down, and kaeshi and nuki techniques when his cut is almost there.

Using the sansappo to order techniques in this way helps me to put them into a framework, but there are a number of other useful ways to understand the theory of timing and opportunity. The concept of Sen, Sen no Sen and Go no Sen is equally effective. This relates to striking before your opponent does, as he starts to strike and finally after he starts his attack.

Another way to think about it is by putting yourself in your opponent's place. In this case, the Shikai or four sicknesses of surprise, fear, doubt and confusion (kyo, ku, gi, waku) can be exploited as attacking opportunities.

With kendo's long history, successive generations of teachers have given us the basis to understand how and why we do things. The challenge for most of us, though, is not to understand the theory but to put it into practice. In this case the answer is "more keiko".

52

Seme and Tame revisited

I have written about seme and tame several times since I started this blog and I feel motivated to do so again. These are difficult concepts for many people to understand and it is even more difficult to translate them into physical action.

We have had numerous conversations about seme at my local dojo, and before writing this I scanned some of the comments on the web relating to this subject. I came across a very interesting thread on Kendo World Forums that started with a post about making seme and waiting for the opponent to react, and how this did not work against more experienced opponents. Obviously the poster is on the right track, but perhaps the clue to why it's not working is in the word "waiting". The missing ingredient is "tame". If you step into striking distance without maintaining the spirit to attack then it is more than likely that you will be the loser in the encounter.

Thinking through the whole process, you should take a big breath in and let half the air out as kakegoe before stepping into your opponent's space. Your attitude should be confident and aggressive with the aim of breaking his physical and mental defence (migamae and kigamae). Posture needs to be correct, with your hips engaged, and you should swiftly pull your left foot up as soon as you step forward with your right. The left heel should be slightly off the ground throughout and there should be a feeling of tension at the back of the left knee. The right knee should be slightly bent. If, while doing this, your opponent's kamae breaks under the pressure, don't wait, just attack.

If, on the other hand, your opponent maintains his guard, you need to take further action to create an opportunity. This is done by keeping an attacking mind and centring your breath in your abdomen. You maintain the pressure in your left foot and knee and, by moving the tip of your shinai very slightly, invite him to attack. As soon as he starts an attacking movement, you can push off from your left foot and make a small sharp strike to whichever target he shows. Use the remainder of the air in your tanden to make a big kiai as you strike either kote or men. Welcome to the world of debana waza.

The Kendo World thread went on to say that it was difficult to make effective seme against more experienced kenshi. Duh, why wouldn't it be? They have been doing it better for a longer time. You will also find it difficult against beginners who have not yet refined their basic technique to a level where they can make "mind contact".

With these less experienced players you can practise tame by building pressure then relaxing it for them to attack you. With seniors, if all else fails, do kakarigeiko.

The Author

Geoff Salmon holds the grade of 7th dan and is one of the few westerners to have passed the new All Japan Kendo Federation kyoshi examination. He spent three years studying kendo in Japan in the 1970s and regularly visits to further his training.

Geoff teaches kendo in the UK and throughout Europe. He has held a number of key kendo posts including that of Chairman of the British Kendo Association and Manager of the British National Kendo Squad. He was a director of the 12th World Kendo Championship in Scotland where he had the honour of welcoming Her Majesty Queen Elizabeth and HRH the Duke of Edinburgh.

Geoff is familiar with high-level kendo as a competitor and referee, with four recent appearances at the Kyoto Taikai to add to his track record of earlier competition in the European and World Championships. He has been a referee at numerous European Championships and at the 15th World Kendo Championships in 2012. Geoff is an active blogger, www.kendoinfo.net and the author of Kendo, A Comprehensive Guide to Japanese Swordsmanship.

In his spare time he is a partner in a headhunting firm and lives in Surrey in the UK.

Made in United States
North Haven, CT
26 April 2022